FALL RISK
A COLLECTION OF POETRY AND SHORT STORIES

NIALL POWER

**MICHELKIN | ** PUBLISHING
ROSWELL, NEW MEXICO
BOOKS.MICHELKIN.COM

Other titles from Michelkin Publishing:

Fighting Against Gravity by Rutherford Rankin
The Charming Swindler by Jeff Musillo
The Knower by Ilan Herman
Dear Sun, Dear Moon by Deborah Paggi & Gayle Cole
Small Boy, Big Dreams by Jeff Musillo & Bryce Prevatte
Gypsies of New Rochelle by Ivan Jenson
Adventures Through the Trees by Kay Gehring
The Ruined Man by Jason DeGray
Irreparable by Jennifer Tucker & Rutherford Rankin
Fanny on Fire by Edith G. Tolchin
Wish Upon A Lantern by Lindy Lorenz & Beth Kruziki
3 of a Kind by Jeff Musillo
The Dark Goddess: Book Two of The Ruined Man Series by Jason DeGray

ISBN: 0-9995222-3-X
ISBN-13: 978-0-9995222-3-3

For Stephen Simon

Acknowledgments

A special thank you to J. Villalobos. This book wouldn't exist without your hard work and love.

Thank you:
Jeff Musillo for wholeheartedly believing in me from the beginning.
Rutherford Rankin and everyone at Michelkin for making this a reality.
My brothers in AA for loving me until I could learn to love myself.
My mother, my father, and Patty for everything.

*"Let everything happen to you: Beauty and terror.
Just keep going. No feeling is final."*

-Rainer Maria Ridge

TABLE OF CONTENTS

BEAUTIFUL

Wouldn't it be beautiful
if I could stay this way,
in this room?
With a good book
and two dogs.
A hot meal
and free porn.
Some cigarettes
and a Bukowski,
looking at all the stars around me.
No need for a woman,
and far from perfection.
Fourth quarter, game seven.
A hot shower and clean laundry.
No booze and no drugs,
no god and no one.
Content on living with deep blues.
Wouldn't it be beautiful
if I grow old enough
to hate my tattoos?

RATS

Her copper hair and her bloody
ankles
as she smiles at the rats.
I smile at her and she catches me
and looks at me like I'm creepy.
Takes off her sweater
and ties up her hair.
Drops her lipstick on the platform,
my hope is reborn.
Not for me
and not for her.
She looks like a bitch
and maybe I am a creep,
but a hope that maybe tonight
I'll be able to sleep.

FALL RISK

Are any of these women real?

My stepmom opens the top drawer
in the guest room,
Takes out the cut-up bracelet
and asks,
"Can I please throw this out?"
It reads, "Fall Risk,"
which is what I am,
Yellowed and frayed
at the ends.

The boxes of books dance with
the lids closed.
It's not cold
but it's raining.
I have one friend and
she's praying.
There are two dogs and
they're saying,
"Please get out of bed,
we believe that you can
walk again."

Fast forward and I get lost
in the big rows, poetry lanes,
while I shake and crave
through the outrages.
I learn to come back down,
I learn to give and go.

It says Fall Risk.
Inside, they told me I'm not bad,
I'm just sick.
It's tricky, whether
I know it all or
have no clue
it exists.
I'm a fall risk.

ALONE

I started sleeping with my clean laundry. It was the first strange thing I did to deal with my loneliness. I came home from the laundromat, took out the fresh, folded batch, and dumped it out on the side of the bed she used to sleep on. Before this, I had done all the customary things one does when newly single.

I downloaded dating apps on my phone, I awkwardly left my number on receipts for waitresses and baristas, I texted girls I used to date years ago, and I watched an unhealthy amount of porn. But with the laundry thing, I felt like I was doing something bizarre. I tossed and turned with it all night, finding myself feeling the different textures of the materials in my fingers, pretending they were little friends of mine, as if they were separate entities, almost like pets. On the third night, I caught myself talking to a pair of boxers that felt good in my hands. Afterwards, I collected the garments and put them back into their drawers.

After she left, I checked myself into rehab. It was my third time. When I got out, I had no idea how to meet people sober. The lack of social lubrication and my exponential fear of rejection led me to a place where I couldn't even talk to a woman.

It had been more than eight months since she left when I resorted to sleeping with my laundry. She had moved on and I had started lying to my friends and family saying I had, too. It seemed the further I got away from being with her, the harder it was to adjust to the fact I was alone. I watched this couple on the train one morning while I was heading to work. He was holding her and kissing her forehead. Her hand was in his back pocket. They were laughing. It seemed foreign to me. It didn't feel like something I had ever done, and it certainly didn't seem like something I would ever do again. I had created an existence that was bringing me further away from intimacy every moment. A negative state of mind that was burying me deeper into loneliness. I was panicking. Years went by like this. Then, I met Felly.

To bridge the gap between sleeping with laundry to meeting Felly, I will explain that nothing happened. I worked in a warehouse, I bought many rotisserie chickens from the supermarket, I watched the entirety of shows I could stream online, whether I enjoyed them or not, and I went to twelve-step meetings. On the surface, I was living a simple, sober, comfortable life. My family was happy, and my friends were not worried. I showed up to the occasional party, I drank club soda, and I smiled. I said things were "pretty good." And honestly, things were not bad. I made it seem like I wasn't lonely. My finest tool was lying. I lied to people about having casual relationships that had come and gone since I had last seen them. I lied to them and I lied to myself.

There's a difference between solitude and loneliness. I was lonely. I was lonely for the first time in my life. I had been in two long-term relationships that took up the entirety of my twenties, had been a popular kid in high school, and had a big family as a kid. I felt pain in the contrast between never being alone and being completely alone. There are different kinds of loneliness like there are different kinds of happiness. I was not worried about my loneliness when it bothered me, when it made me uncomfortable and made me do strange things. It was when I became okay with it that I started to worry. I was losing emotion through detachment, and I was starting to revel in it. There was a strength in detachment, a power in not being able to be let down by another person. I couldn't be hurt by what I could no longer feel. Still, sometimes I craved it. The way a woman smelled up close, the way one's skin felt, these sensations began to move away from me. But as time passed, I missed it less and less and that made me more and more afraid.

Most days I would have this quiet pride in being untouchable by loss, but other days I would feel desperate for interaction. Desperation is interesting. Desperation is why my girlfriend left. Desperation is what got me sober. It is also the reason I signed up to volunteer at the rehab on Sundays. I was both desperate and unable to talk to people. At the regular AA meetings, I couldn't bring myself to talk to anyone. Speaking was voluntary, and socializing was no different in those rooms than it was out in the world. The deeper I got into my social destruction, the harder it was to get my hand up and share or to put my hand out and introduce myself.

Volunteering at the rehab, I had to speak. All week long I looked forward to being there. Along with complicity in desolation, a new curious condition had formed in me—the sadness, the hopelessness of the rehab, I enjoyed it. It made me feel alive. Was I helping? Was it helping me? I don't know. If anyone asked, those were the reasons I went, but like I have already explained—I lied a lot.

At some point in my sobriety, I met Eddie. He was twenty-seven years sober. He was married. He had adult children. He owned a business. He was social. He was happy. He was everything I was not. He was the one who introduced me to meetings at the rehab. We would get coffee beforehand and I would lie to him about the girls I was casually dating and the things I was doing for fun in my spare time. I enjoyed being around Eddie. I fantasized over his normality. I observed his mannerisms and imitated them in front of my family.

One day he didn't show up to speak with me at the rehab. I called him afterward and he didn't answer. It wasn't until four weeks later that I saw Eddie again. He was a patient there. His hair was greasy and there were bags under his eyes. Capillaries were broken around his face. It was a shock to see him sitting in the patient circle when I walked into the common area that Sunday evening. He didn't seem embarrassed or ashamed sitting there. He simply nodded to me and I began to speak.

Once I finished speaking, he put his hand up. " My daughter is dead." His daughter, Felicity, had overdosed. Eddie had shown me pictures of Felly (what he called her) before. Her pronounced jawline. Her high cheekbones and long neck. Her pale blue eyes and thin blond hair. She overdosed on a mixture of Xanax and alcohol, the combination I once so enjoyed. She was thirty-two years old, the same age I was that day. She had been sober for almost four years before she relapsed, the same amount of time I had been sober sitting in the front of the room that evening. Eddie had told me these things about his daughter before, but it wasn't until I sat there listening to him talking about her overdose that I recognized all the similarities between us. I suddenly felt intensely connected to her. Looking back on it, it was because she was also alone now. We had everything in common.

As Eddie spoke, the room drew into his sadness. I did not. I completely overlooked how my friend was feeling. I couldn't come close to thinking about his struggle, his grief. All I could think about was my lost opportunity of meeting Felly. I had become preoccupied with this guttural connection to her. Eddie went on about his relapse and how he was going to go away to a long-term inpatient program upstate. His voice sounded like it was coming from a different room. My eyes blurred out my surroundings. I felt paralyzed like I needed to be shaken physically to snap out of it. After the meeting, we hugged and he cried. I felt embarrassed for him. I wished him luck with rehab. I don't know if I meant it. I no longer cared about Eddie. I only cared about one thing, and that one thing was meeting Felly.

I spoke to Eddie in private before I left the rehab. I asked if there was anything I could do. "Stay sober," was his response. Addicts can be so fucking cliché. I told him that I wanted to pay my respects, that it was the least I could do. He told me she was buried in Staten Island, only a short bus ride away from my apartment in Brooklyn. If it wasn't 10:00 p.m. on a Sunday, I would have gone straight there.

I wanted to be around her, to be with her. I recognized how illogical that was. I could not, and still cannot, explain what my expectations were. I told myself that it was just curiosity, a desire to show myself how things may have ended for me had I not sobered up. I even tried to tell myself that it was sincerity, that I did want to pay respects. I couldn't sit with that sentiment for more than a few seconds. All I knew was that I had to go. I had to see the flowers on the plot. I had to see her picture surrounded by memorabilia from her life, knickknacks placed there by friends symbolizing inside jokes, a childhood toy, anything. I had to speak out loud to her, standing over her body.

I could barely sleep that night. The street light that shined into my bedroom never bothered me before, but that night I played with my curtain, unable to block out the shine that lit up the foot of my bed and glared off my mirror. I would doze off for a little while then wake up, wishing the light was the morning so I could get up and head out.

I took a personal day from work and caught the 7:15 a.m. bus to Staten Island. While crossing over the Verrazano Bridge, I could see the skyline in the distance and looked at the piers extended off Bay Ridge by my apartment. It was a rainy morning and I had never been to Staten Island before. The cemetery was a short walk from where I got off the bus. Eddie had given me her full name and directions to her grave. It was easily recognizable. Only a couple of weeks old, the plot was covered in flowers and cards. I didn't think to bring either. I saw a single purple flower laid in front of some random grave I walked passed and I picked it up. It didn't feel right to show up empty-handed.

I stood over her silently for a few minutes. There were dozens of bouquets and pictures surrounding the tombstone. There was a picture of her and a girlfriend posing with their arms around each other's waists that stood out to me. She looked inviting. I found myself wanting to have my arm around her waist. She was not beautiful, but she was uniquely intriguing. Her blonde hair fell half over her gray-blue eyes. She was tall, probably taller than I am, and she was skinny. Her lips and nose were small but pronounced. Her unevenness made her strangely sexy. There was a professional portrait of her next to it, probably a class photo. It looked like a different person altogether.

Standing there, my loneliness hit its pinnacle. The reason for my trip had become clear. I wanted to meet someone who was more alone than I was. I wanted to feel good about myself, feel good that I was at least alive. But what I felt was jealousy. I envied Felly for being dead. I was stuck trying to figure out this isolation. I crumpled up the flower in my hand and dropped it in front of the grave. "Fuck you," was all I managed to exhale as I turned back towards the bus stop.

It was still early when I got back to my place, but my day was done. The rest of that day I smoked cigarettes and watched porn and mindless television. At 9:00 p.m., hours before I would typically go to bed, I turned off the lights and lay down. I wasn't tired, but I didn't want to be awake.

When I woke up, she was sitting at the edge of my bed looking down at her hands. The street light came in from outside and lit up her face so perfectly there was no question whether it was her or not. As improbable as it may seem, it didn't seem all that crazy to me at the time. I knew it wasn't a dream, that wasn't even a question. I was awake. My focus first went to the indentation of her sitting on the bed. This was no translucent figure. She saw that I was no longer sleeping, and she turned shyly and looked up at me through her thin, greasy hair then back down at her hands. I propped myself onto my elbows and decided to break the silence.

"Hi, Felly. It's nice to meet you."

"Hi." She paused for a moment. "I'm sorry if I'm bothering you. And I'm sorry it's so late. I didn't think you would be asleep." I looked at the clock, it was 1:13 a.m.

"No, it's okay, really," I said, sitting up in a little more. "I, I just wasn't feeling great, so I went to bed early. I'm usually up at this time." I swung my feet around and placed them on the floor. When I did so, my foot grazed the side of her leg. It was confirmed. She was solid. I picked up a t-shirt off the floor and stood up. Besides the light coming in from outside, the room was dark.

"I know we don't know each other, but I was hoping we could talk. I saw you today at my grave. I saw how angry you were. I know who you are even though we have never met. You mean a lot to my dad, and I'm worried about him. I just thought maybe if you—"

"Felly," I interrupted. "Can I turn on the light?" She paused for a few seconds then nodded that it was okay. I walked over and flipped on the light. Once my eyes adjusted, I got my first real look at her. Her features had a different effect in person. She had that sharp unevenness to her, and a gauntness, but face to face there was a seductive quality I didn't get from the pictures. She looked over and made eye contact with me for the first time. Her eye sockets were dark. She looked like she had been outside for a while. Her hair didn't look like it had been washed in weeks and her clothes were dirty. "Listen, Felly. I do want to know why you are here and everything, I can tell you how Eddie is doing and all that, but first, let me just wake up a little bit. I'm going to put on some coffee. I don't have any beer or anything. Coffee is the best I can do."

7

"Coffee would be nice, yeah. And, don't worry about that. I think I am going to stay back on the wagon for now. I've been sober since I died and that was almost four weeks ago now, so we both know the hardest part is over." She looked at me and forced out a smile. "While you do that, can I use the bathroom? Freshen up some?"

"Of course." I opened the bedroom door and pointed to the left. "Wait, take some clean clothes." I handed her a pair of sweatpants and my favorite blue hoodie which were strewn on the couch in my room.

After I made two coffees, we sat on the couch. She had showered and was now wearing my clothes. Her hair was wet, and the clothes hung off her narrow frame. It would have seemed completely normal, like two living people sitting together for coffee, if only there wasn't a cool breeze emanating from her skin.

"Sorry. I don't have any sugar."

"It's fine. I usually drink it black anyway." She sipped her coffee and rolled up the sleeves of the sweatshirt and the cuffs of the sweatpants.

"Are you warm?"

"Yeah, but it's fine, really."

"That's funny, because you have like, a cold breeze kind of coming off your body. It feels like a light fan or something." She said nothing like she didn't hear me. I sipped my coffee. "I'm sorry I said, 'Fuck you,' to your grave today. It wasn't about you. It's just, I'm having a tough time lately, I—"

"I know. It's fine." She sipped her coffee and wiped the sweat from her forehead with the shoulder of the hoodie and readjusted the sleeves up past the elbow and the pant legs up past the knee. "How is my dad?"

"Um...he's in rehab. He's having a tough time with all this, ya know?"

"Oh." She looked back down. "I have never seen him drink before. He got sober when I was very young." I noticed her eyes were filling up with tears. She was sweating so much I couldn't tell if a tear was falling down her face or if it was another bead of sweat. Her face was turning red.

"We should talk about something else. Maybe something lighter? We can talk about all this stuff another time."

"I'm sorry. I need to take this off. Is that okay?" She tugged at the hoodie.

"Of course." She grabbed the bottom of the sweatshirt and pulled it up. When she raised her arms over her head, I could see her rib cage, followed by her smooth underarms and her collarbone. She then slid the pants down in one motion and took two quick steps out of the legs. As each article came off and more skin was exposed, the cool breeze coming off her grew stronger. There was definition in her legs. You could see where the muscles were attached to the bones. She was thin enough that her thighs never touched creating a gap extending all the way up to her crotch. My heart began to race. She looked over at me and it was obvious that I was examining her body. In trying not to, I only made it more obvious that I was looking.

"Do you mind if I just sleep for a few hours and we can talk in the morning?" she asked apologetically.

"Of course not. Take my bed. I'll sleep on the couch. You must be exhausted." She paused for a few seconds and then nodded. I went into the kitchen and got two glasses of water. I put ice in hers. I put the other one by the couch and handed her the one with ice.

"Do you have a fan?" she asked, looking embarrassed. I did. I turned it on and directed it towards the bed. I walked over and turned off the light. We lay in silence and I stared at the ceiling knowing I wouldn't be able to sleep.

"Sleep next to me," she blurted out, courageously, in one breath. I didn't say anything. I just waited a few seconds and moved towards the bed. I could feel her breathing and I felt the cold air against my skin. After trying to bear it for a few minutes, I sat up and put on the discarded clothes she had taken off earlier. She kicked the blankets off herself.

"Are you still warm?"

"Yeah. I think my body is just adjusting to all the changes. Do I really feel cold to you?" I touched her arm and even though she gave off a cool air, her skin felt normal.

"You feel fine. I guess death has a strange effect on people. Different for those who are experiencing it than those who are witnessing it. Let me try something. Tell me if you want me to stop." I leaned over her and picked the glass of ice water up off the floor. I poured a very small amount into my other palm and I let it drip onto her neck. I did it again onto her stomach and again on her legs. I took out a piece of ice and rubbed it against her skin directly. She didn't stop me. She kept her eyes closed and let out a light moan. After a minute she slid her hand up my shirt after giving me the go-ahead I needed. I dripped the cold water under her bra and down her the front of her underwear and let my hand follow. Before long, I was kissing her neck and her chest. Goosebumps were running up and down my entire body. There was an intense cold coming from her. She never told me to stop.

9

Felly didn't leave after that night. The conversation of whether she would stay or go was never had. From then on out, she was just there. I had spent years perfecting being alone. It didn't take long with her being there for the idea of being alone again to terrify me. If what I was looking for that day I visited her grave was an escape from loneliness, I had accomplished that.

Things started off great. She was everything I could hope for in a partner. She was sexual, she could relate to my problems with addiction, and she couldn't leave me. Every relationship I'd had before Felly, I lived in constant anxiety that they would leave me. She couldn't because she had nowhere to go. She couldn't face the outside world because the outside world couldn't face her. It wasn't all easy. When it came to sex, there was this issue of our temperatures, so I would place the fan to the side of her, put ice in a plastic baggie and rub it on her chest and neck while I knelt in front of her in a hoodie. She would stay in my apartment while I was at work, read my books, and watch TV. When I would get home at night we would usually take a walk down to the pier. She would wear only a t-shirt and shorts even though it was winter. This was what she looked forward to all day. She would stand at the edge of the pier and look up at the bridge letting the cold air run over her skin. Some nights we would have great conversations, other nights we wouldn't talk at all.

One night, while down there, I asked her about her relapse and eventual overdose.

"What happened? What made you go back to using?"

"My boyfriend left me. I met him when I was only a few weeks sober, only a couple of days out of rehab, and he was with me the whole time. Then, three and a half years later he told me he was in love with someone else. Before I could even wrap my head around it, he was living with her. I couldn't handle it." I didn't reply right away. I could see that just talking about it made her body temperature rise. I could see the steam rising into the cold air. While she spoke, I thought about consequences.

"So, would you say your mistake was dating someone too early into your sobriety?"

"No. My mistake was trying to be happy."

"Sorry?"

"I realized this in the moments right before I died. People are constantly trying to be happy, and that's where the problem lies. Not just for me, but for most people."

"So, you don't think people should try to be happy?"

"I don't think it really exists. I think when we do it we are

10

chasing something that we won't be able to find. Or if we find it, we'll then lose it and be further away from it than we ever were. It's a dangerous exploration. It killed me, and I believe it kills a lot of people, most people." I didn't argue with her.

For a while, things went smoothly for Felly and me. I can say our arrangement made me happy. And to Felly's point, this became a problem. The happiness of having someone waiting for me at home was making me less detached than I had been. At my AA meetings, I was beginning to feel empathy for people again. It was uncomfortable. I liked where I was before. It had taken time to get there and I didn't want to lose that. There is a comfort in being disconnected, a safety. What I feared most was that I would start to really care again. And the happiness I'd gain, I'd eventually lose. So, I was faced with a dilemma: was I going to try and be happy, or was I going to be okay, safe? There were other problems, too. I felt that a seal had been broken now that I had been with someone. I found myself lusting over random women, not from a place of visceral necessity, but from a place of intrigue and variety. But there could be no straying, no testing the waters. The problem was that my relationship was not your normal one—my girlfriend was dead. She had nowhere else to go.

She was also dependent on me. She couldn't go out with friends and give us a night off from each other. She couldn't even go out and buy herself food. Additionally, there was this issue of her cooling herself down. There were places she could not reach with ice, and according to her, when she tried to rub herself down with cool rags or cold water, she would never gain the same effect as when I did it. Temperature was an issue on both sides. I was becoming affected by our situation too. At night I had to sleep with a heating blanket and would wake up drenched in sweat. My ears and nose were always red and hot from the temperature changes and I had developed a constantly running nose and a hollow cough. My coworkers thought I had pneumonia.

Then there were the more typical problems. Felly became jealous. When I would talk about a female friend, her enthusiasm for the story would diminish. When I would want to make plans that took me outside of our routine she would sulk while telling me it was fine, that nothing was wrong. On top of that, the sex was becoming more routine by the day. The edgy mechanics that aroused me in the beginning were starting to feel like a chore. Our conversations were being repeated. We were not gaining any experiences outside of ourselves to bring to the table. If I brought this up, she would get defensive and self-conscious about being dead. I didn't have the heart to tell her that her lack of life was ruining what we had. And this compassion was showing me that I was quickly losing what I had worked so hard to obtain by being lonely, that disconnect I had before I met her.

The months passed. She went from an inconvenience to a major problem for me. I would often think back to my conversation with Felly about happiness. I disagreed with her. If she could not find happiness, that was her problem. I had never been able to find it either, but the more I thought about it, the more I started to think that maybe I could find it one day. That maybe I had it when I was alone. When she came to me, I thought I needed someone, anyone, to be with. But being alone, you don't need anything. You're free. I knew she wouldn't respond well to a practical conversation about this, but I figured it couldn't hurt to try.

I couldn't get much out before the theatrics began. While she was having her tantrum, I realized I had made a giant mistake. She bashed everything about me. She attacked my physical appearance, my insecurities, my fears, my doubts, my past, everything. No one ever spoke to me the way Felly did that night. She ended her tirade with, "Now I see why she left you. You know what? I've seen it all along. You're pathetic. If I was alive I would have left months ago. Do you think if I was alive I would have ever even come to you?"

I left the apartment and found myself sitting at a bar. I had been sober more than four years at this point. I ordered a beer and a whiskey neat. I sat staring at the drinks. The bartender was looking over at me, then away, then back at me. After about twenty minutes or so he asked, "Are you waiting for someone?" I just shook my head and continued to gaze at the full glasses.

After a while, it dawned on me that this was not worth giving up all I had worked for. I would rather find a way to get out of this relationship than ruin my sobriety. I left a twenty on the bar, the drinks untouched, and left. I set out for home but made two stops before returning to my apartment. When I got back to my place she was sitting on my couch, wearing one of my t-shirts and a pair of my boxers.

"Where were you?"

"At a bar." She stood up, and I saw tears fill her eyes.

"No. No. I'm sorry. I didn't mean those things. I swear. I just—"

"I didn't drink, Felly. I almost did. But I didn't."

"Thank God. I just want you to know I—"

"It's okay." I sat down on the bed. "I care about you, Felly. I want this to work, but this situation is toxic. We need to figure out how we can both have lives."

"Well, I'm dead. I'm sorry it is such an inconvenience to you. But there is nothing I can do about that now."

"I know. But I was thinking, maybe there is another way we could make this right."

"Like?"

"What if we were both dead?" She stared at me in disbelief.

"You would do that for me?"

"I would do that for us. I have nothing here. You're all I have." She jumped off the couch and embraced me. She held me tighter than I knew she was capable of. Then she whispered in my ear.

"I have never been so happy in my entire afterlife."

I told her we should walk down to the pier and talk about how we would go about it. It was a snowy February night. Felly wore a light jacket to avoid drawing attention to herself. I was freezing, even all bundled up. I held her hand and between her and the weather I could barely keep my teeth from chattering. I was so tired of being cold. She kept looking over at me and smiling. I would force a fake smile back. Each time, it got harder to do.

We sat on a bench looking out over at the half-frozen Hudson. Sledges of ice crawled down the river.

"Are you cold?" she asked. I was breathing into my hands.

"Freezing," I managed to chatter out. "I—I'm sure you're warm, right?"

"Of course," she said with a little annoying chuckle.

"Well, nobody is down here. Take off the jacket. I'll rub some snow on you." She took off the jacket and sat there in her tank top, facing the water with her back to me. She spread out her skinny arms and put her head back, collecting the snow on her tongue. I sat behind her and with my numb, red hands started rubbing snow on her neck. The blue lights from the bridge glistened off the icy water, creating a silver haze all around her.

"Close your eyes. Think of how nice it will be when we are both dead together." She closed her eyes and as she did I reached under the bench we'd been purposefully sitting on. Between the bar and going back to the apartment I had stopped at the gas station. There I purchased a gas can and fifteen dollars' worth of gas. I left the can open under the bench knowing that there would only be a few seconds before Felly would realize what was happening. I lifted the can over her bent back head and started to pour. Like I had predicted, I was only able to pour the gas on her for a moment before she jerked forward in her seat. She coughed and gasped while I stood up and continued to soak her with gas. I lit the book of matches and tossed them over her shoulder, down the front of her shirt. I had anticipated awful shrieking, but I was wrong. For a brief, terrifying second I thought it wasn't going to work, that you couldn't burn the dead. But then she started to burn. Once she caught fire, she just stood up calmly, turned around, and looked at me. All I received from her in the form of a reaction was a look of disappointment. Then the flames reached her face.

Though she ignited over her chest, once she was engulfed, it was her feet that began crumble and fade away first, leaving her looking ethereal, and for the first time like a ghost. In these short moments, I thought about what it was to be alone. I realized that I had been no more alone in the years leading up to meeting Felly than I had been the years I was with my ex. I had always been alone, and I would always be alone. At the same time, I have never been alone. I never would be alone. There was no such thing. Alone is a fictional, human invention.

I was standing downwind from where she was burning. The warm air and ash were blowing all over me. The heat on my skin made the flakes of snow melt upon contact. I closed my eyes and enjoyed the comforting breeze. I was only able to enjoy the warmth for a few minutes. Then she was gone.

When I got home, I stood and looked in the full-length mirror. The front of my clothes was covered in ash. I took them off and placed them on the side of the bed where Felly had slept. I took a nice, long, hot shower, and when I got out I was exhausted. I turned off the lights and I lay in my bed next to the clothes.

THE LEAVING SEASON

This is the leaving season.
Emergency vehicles
heading in opposite directions
for different reasons.

The middle of my cigarette
was the end of one man's life.
Cut lines and a dropped call,
the rise in the blacktop,
and the places she never called home.

A girl skips on the sidewalk,
oranges fall from the market,
small obstacles in the path
of strong legs moved by imagination.
Fantasies of what normal feels like,
routines of a year ago forgotten.
Did I drink coffee in the morning?
Did I always wake up in pain?
Are him and I the same?

Last night I felt it.
Something was coming,
something awful.
Or, even worse,
nothing at all.

SPOILED

Spoiled
West Highland Terriers.
Man, they're everywhere.
Pulling back on leashes.
Giving us humans
that look
as if we've mistook
what time is and
the value of the smell that is
right now.

TIME MACHINE

If I could go back in time,
I wouldn't change a thing I've done
or didn't do.
I wouldn't stay in the night I met you.

I would travel to the time of the beats.
How nice it is to imagine "leaving town"
with no traces
except the ones I choose.

To live in a motel,
come and go as I please.
Smoke cigarettes and drink beer,
eat the food without the junk.

Wander to different towns,
taking odd jobs.
Meeting different women.
They don't have to be beautiful.

Never getting too close
or too familiar.
Putting out my thumb,
never getting left behind.

I don't need big lights
or white beaches.
Give me American small towns
and their niches.

In a time people still ramble.
To live offline,
call home from a phone with a cord
and say, "I'm doing fine."

HOTEL ROOM

Sometimes, things are there we cannot see.
They are hidden in the dark.
I'm reminded of when time was clean,
when we made love, and it was not routine.

What came next took my breath.
I got up. And you just left.
I had on my boots
but this was no footnote.

I took to whiskey,
Xanax, and cocaine
and mostly just
self-pity.
I disappeared for sixty days
from myself, from everyone else.
Like a man on an island
trapped behind his eyelids.

Then I saw something I could never see.
I saw me.

OVERSIZED

Oversized,
like only it can be in a dream.
Which is where you came back to me
and I felt the need
to tell you how beautiful
you are to me.
In between
the haunted sidewalk
cafes.
Near the deep blues
that were left for you.
Like the feeling remembered
of a thought forgotten.

CYNICAL

She reads Agatha Christie,
taking breaks
to imagine what the weather is like
in France.

She opens the window to feel the storm.
I imagine her glasses fog up
and when she blinks,
her lashes clean them like windshield wipers.

She's cynical about love
and foreign to the touch.
She shuts out all the lust
that's range. Porcelain to dust.
When she is overcome,
it's with a demon
from a console,
raging to life like a tantrum.

If I could have her any way,
I'd take her covered in fake blood
in the foyer of a haunted house,
mounted in a ripped-up blouse,
her lips matching the color
of the dye in her hair.
Dip my romantic in her cynicism.
Keep the window open to let the city listen.

RUN TOWARDS CHAOS

We run towards chaos
We thought we were gods
We fought odds
and took you with us
Left you alone
without a lie to trust
We forced lust
we made you scream
To us
nothing was what it would seem
For us
it was all a bad dream

THINGS I ONCE FOUND BEAUTIFUL

Things I once found beautiful,
like not knowing when I saw you
on that rooftop
that I would love you.
When we'd walk down Riverside
in all seasons.
You telling me about
Boston and Outer Space.

Sleeping on airplanes.
Talking about
books and my dead friends
with whiskey and champagne,

are now painful reminders
being replaced with a blindness,
a bloody tongue on an outlet,
lighting a fire in a fountain.

WRITE

I write to you for a
difference of opinion.
To be kept in the dark,
far away from His wisdom.

You,
like a tripped wire
in a bone structure prison.
You,
dancing through rooms
in and out of perfect vision.

The news of distant killings
and tortured women
is proof they're all the same
and we're something different.

There is a fire between the pages,
a story for the ages.

You say, "Just keep them coming."
I tell you what you already knew.
God created truth so
I could lie to you.

FUCKIN' HOT OUT

Fuck. This. Shit.
Those brief moments of unrequited anger that come muddled in with
vast hopelessness.
That's it. I'll hate trains forever. They will all be delayed. I'll always be
running late.
They had the party and they promised they would love each other
until one died. He'll love her forever. She'll move on eventually. But
this afternoon, they fight on the train. The main reason? It's fuckin'
hot out.
Lay at the end of the day. We are just people. This is just life.
I left the house without my medicine. Yet again.

STRANGER

You are most beautiful when you yawn.
When your nose crackles behind
your glasses.
And your eyes are blood red from
the dawn.

A complete savage act of passion.
A greasy-haired lack of action.
Wearing a stained
white labored napkin.
You make tired look like a statement of fashion.

Then you left me like
nothing happened.
Withdrawn from me and all these simple bastards.
You were never real and this
never mattered.
I'll remember your teeth in my
broken ashtray.

DOG DAY DREAM

A dog doesn't need a glass of wine
to unwind.
Or a good book.
Or a cold beer.
To escape, it just wants you
to let it escape
with a walk.
A dog's imagination is the dirt and the smell
of the grass and the flowers.
I spent half a year without
being touched
by a human.

XANAX

When I bring them home
I lay them out on the desk
and inspect them
one by one
Twelve pills
Broke in half
that's twenty-four
nights sleep
But
let's celebrate tonight
take one and a half
and order Thai food

Seven days later
a fresh batch
I get three dozen
Half of one at 4:00
another half at 8:00
a full one at midnight
One when I'm tired
One when I'm wired
An extra one for anger
A backup few for pain
And of course—a secret stash
for if I go insane

They're there so I can prove
to her
I can sleep
that I don't need to drink
So I can prove to myself
that I don't need to drink

Comes the time
when routine gets
shut off
Where I end and
they begin
There is no more plan
My life's in their hands

A WEEKEND, 2009

Open on a cool September day
where the sun gives you the chills.
It could have been the girls
or it could have been the pills.

I got my hair cut
then we went to the park.
We preceded
to drink until it was dark.

Little did I know
what was hiding underneath.
You can't be scared of something,
something you can't see.

When I woke up,
I wondered what had happened.
Life seemed to have changed
in such an ordinary fashion.

I got out of bed,
I felt healthy and tall.
I popped a few more pills
and went to watch football.

BLACK BAGS

Dividend.
The dust bowl dance of a cigarette.
Black trash bags and it's evident.
 The white of your eyes
negates the brown of your thighs.
The smell of your breath
masked by the smell of death.

RIOTS

Under the weaponry
of stars and stripes,
Alice let her first son die.
When asked
why she let her
boy go,
she said,
"Why make
another man
to fight,
to fuck,
and not throw out his popcorn
after movies?"
To be the first to
complain
and the last to die.
To be quiet until he's
loud.

EVERYTHING CHANGED

Everything changed
like the rooftops in Queens.
Snow to rain to leaves.
It's never as beautiful as they promised.

The trouble with their baggage.
The lovers with one another.
Time moves differently for them.
A great adventure on just another today.
I can put us in Paris
or by a waterfall in winter.
Put myself here with my pen
knowing it will all change again.

It's always right now.
The only constant is,
I'll always be looking.
I'll never be found.

FIFTH POCKET

The plan was to be at The Wallace at 9:00 p.m. I had set my alarm for 8:15 but wasn't able to get out of my bed until 8:45. Even once I was up, I had to make myself puke, put a cold Pepsi can on my eyes for a few minutes, shower, and smoke a bowl. If I wasn't able to fit all these things in, there was no way I would have been able to make it. I knew once I got to the bar, had a drink or two, let the potions go to work, I would be fine. I tried not to drink too much earlier that afternoon, but when Lila was out of town for work, my afternoon drinks always turned into a few-hour ordeal. Knowing I had to be somewhere later that evening made it even harder to nap. Between three and four, I got up every few minutes to piss. I was having trouble getting myself ready to go. I gave in and took a shot of Evan Williams between bowl rips. The weed wasn't doing the trick and because I hadn't seen Aaron in months and Jimmy in years, I didn't want to look jumpy.

The whole walk there I massaged the outside of the fifth pocket of my jeans. The feeling of the little pill inside was comforting just knowing it was there. The outline of it against my fingers took a little bit of the edge off. Once it was in my mouth a little more of that edge would be gone. When it was washed down I would know the relief was inevitable, and then, of course, the actual relief. I was convinced Xanax was the invention of the most brilliant minds to ever live. My head was still pulsating a little bit. I needed to think of an excuse for being a half hour late. Aaron was coming from the Financial District, and Jimmy had come all the way from Philadelphia. I only had to travel six blocks.

When I got there, I saw them sitting at a high-top table with three barstools. Jimmy and I embraced first. It had been so long since we'd seen each other. He was married now and had a small baby. I hadn't met either of them. He'd filled out in the face and midsection and his hair was thinning.

"Look at you, you preppy fuck!" We hugged and I ruffled his beard.

"How are you? It's been forever. How's Lila?" He held me at my shoulders as he asked.

"She's in D.C. Work. No complaints here."

"So, I'm sure you are hitting the bottle hard, even for you, huh?" Aaron interjected with a smile. I put my arm around his neck, a mixture of a hug and a headlock.

"So, do I order at the bar or do we have a waitress or something?" They had two half glasses of dark beer in front of them. I could tell the beer was rich by the remnants of the foam sticking to the rim of the glasses.

"Some cute girl took our order, but it's pretty busy. I would just go to the bar," Jimmy suggested.

"I'm going to get a whiskey with my beer. Anyone else?"

"No, no, no. I stay away from the hard stuff these days. I'll be on the mend for days if I start drinking whiskey and I'm in town for a meeting tomorrow," Jimmy said, holding his hands to his chest.

"I'm okay for now, too. Maybe later," Aaron added.

As I waited to get the bartender's attention, I played with the pill between my fingers. My mouth watered. I ordered a Jameson neat and a hard cider, no ice. While I watched him make my order, I slid the pill under my tongue. I felt the chalky pill turn gooey and silky. The taste was dull, yet bitter. I sipped the cider, letting it dissolve in the sparkling liquid. Then I threw back the entire whiskey, which was meant to be sipped, and took a couple of hard gulps of the cider with my eyes closed. I pointed to the empty highball and gave a thumbs-up to the bartender. He filled it up and I walked back over to the table with a full whiskey and three-fourths of a cider. I was eager to order something to eat, something salty to snack on. The first thirty minutes of a Xanax high was the only time I was able to eat.

When I got back to the table, Aaron and Jimmy were still nursing their first beers. My return seemed to murder their conversation. Before I could address the sudden silence, Jimmy put his hairy hand on my shoulder and squeezed it.

"So man, what's new with you? I want to hear it all." I was scanning the floor for our waitress so I could order food. It had suddenly dawned on me that I hadn't eaten anything since last night. When I woke up that morning there was a half-eaten sandwich on my bedroom floor.

"Not too much, man. It's a slow time of year for the bar and Lila is out of town. I did start watching *Oz* on HBO. You guys seen it? It's fuckin' rad." Aaron had a full mouth of beer but groaned in agreement.

"The bar, man. God, I miss that place. You're the manager now, right?" Jimmy didn't seem to be interested in the show.

"Well, there is no manager, but I have been there the longest and I make the schedule and do the ordering and shit."

"And how is Lila's job? I heard she's killing it."

"She's doing well."

"You guys been together what, like, it's gotta be at least five years now right?"

"Almost seven."

"Wow...you putting aside a few months' salary for a ring or what?" Aaron could see that I was getting uncomfortable and he quickly changed the subject.

I shot back the rest of my whiskey and finished my glass of cider. I was starting to feel awake. I was starting to feel normal.

"Speaking of big news, why don't you share the info with the rest of the table, J?" Aaron said excitedly.

"Erica is pregnant," Jimmy said, smiling and nodding, looking me in the eyes.

"What?! You guys, like, just had a kid." I immediately realized that I should be acting more elated than surprised and pulled him in for a hug. "That's amazing, man. Proud of you, man."

"Yeah, dude. It's exciting stuff. I can't believe it. It's all happening so fast but, ya know, we want Cody to have a sibling that's close enough in age so they can play sports or whatever together. And we just bought the house, so the timing just makes sense."

"Yeah, you might as well get it all done at once, right?" I said confidently. Jimmy shrugged his shoulders and nodded.

Aaron got up to get another round for the table. I teased him into bringing back shots for the two of us. I didn't bother working the peer pressure on Jimmy.

We sat and drank. We sat and talked—mostly about high school. Aaron and I had been living in New York together since school ended so it was mostly Jimmy catching us up about his life down in Philly. About an hour in, Jimmy got up to use the bathroom and Aaron's demeanor changed.

"Dude, you are slurring like a mother fucker." He took a small glass vial of white powder out of his pocket and handed it to me under the table. "Do a bump. You're getting sloppy. What time did you start drinking?"

"Fuck off," I said, smiling. I stood up and put the vial in my pocket.

"Have you taken any Xanax or anything? Any perks? It's not good to mix that shit."

"Nah, I'm good." Right when Jimmy sat back down, I got up and headed to the bathroom. When I got back, I passed the vial back to Aaron under the table.

At around 11:30, Jimmy announced he was leaving.

"Yeah, yeah, I know, but I have a meeting early tomorrow and I need to be fresh." He said his goodbyes to Aaron, and then it was my turn. "Take care of yourself, man." We hugged. "I worry about you, dude," he added. I was having a little trouble articulating myself at this point. I shot Aaron an irksome look over Jimmy's shoulder.

"Congrats on things. On everything," I mumbled out. As he got to the door, Jimmy turned back over his shoulder and waved at us with a toothless smile—the way you wave to the mailman.

"Can you believe that fuckin' guy? Worry about me?" At this point, I had gone into the bathroom with the vial a few times. My motor skills had improved.

"Yeah dude, I can. You guys are just in different places. And honestly, you do seem a little off the rails lately. Is everything okay with you and Lila?"

"We're not doing this right now, Aaron." I finished my beer and motioned to the waitress to bring us another round. Aaron had done enough blow by then to start in on his conspiracy theory rants. I embraced it; at least he wasn't talking about me. We had a few more drinks.

We decided to go back to my place and smoke some weed. Aaron was one of those guys who claimed he didn't smoke, but at the end of nights like this, he'd always want to go back to my apartment and get high. We sat on my back deck and I rolled a joint. It was a second-story deck that had a long alleyway running off the back of it. The buildings to both the north and south were about ten stories tall, blocking the commotion of the city. A thin slice of the night sky snuck through and when we got out there the moon sat right between the buildings. I poured us a couple of whiskeys and brought out a couple of beers. At this point we were drunk and I decided to bring it up.

"Him of all people. He has some nerve. Just because he has a wife and a couple of kids and I'm still bartending and shit, he thinks he has his shit together. Fuck that. You know what he did. You know what he's really like."

"Yo. We agreed, man."

"So what? It's just us here, right? We're fucked up. I want to talk about it, man." I was animated now. Aaron looked past his glass down the alleyway for a nearly a minute, then slowly started to speak.

"It was...it was so fucked up, man. I still think about it sometimes, honestly. I try not to. It's been a while since we've talked about it. I don't know if we should or not. That shit fucked me up for a while. I'd rather just try and forget."

"Well, you haven't forgotten, and neither have I. We've kept it in for over ten years now. Maybe if we just talk about it for a few minutes tonight, we can just put it behind us." Aaron was now looking down between his feet. The joint had gone out and I started trying to talk as I was lighting it back up. He spoke as I was inhaling.

28

"Do you remember the noise it made when it got hit? The worst noise I've ever heard. And the way it bucked? It's front legs buckling and its neck turning on the floor? Then another shot. That second shot, there was an explosion on it...I saw blood and chunks fly off its back." I saw Aaron had tears in his eyes. I started to think then that maybe I shouldn't have brought it up. I was about to try and change the subject, but it was too late. Aaron was back there, he couldn't stop. "He planned it, man. He called us over and said he had something to show us. I honestly thought he was growing shrooms or something when he started walking us behind that farm. I wanted to stop him, man, but he had that gun. I was like, afraid. The way he looked."

"That's what I think about even more than the noises the horse made." My voice was calmer than Aaron's. "The way Jimmy looked. The look on his face after the first shot. And then after the second shot, when we were begging him to put it out of its misery. He like, waited. He was watching it." We both sat silently for a minute. I felt sober.

"We should have told someone. We should have told that woman."

"Dude, we would have got in trouble. You could have lost your scholarship. And it wouldn't have changed anything."

"Were you afraid of him? Or just of getting in trouble?" When Aaron asked me this, he turned towards me and held eye contact. "Be honest." I looked back at him, then towards my feet, then back at him.

"I guess both." I poured two shots for us, handed him one, tapped my glass against his which sat idly in his hand, and threw mine back. We sat in silence for a couple of minutes. I looked up at the fire escapes and at the windows of the buildings in the alley. The joint was out again.

GOLD

What if this is the
best it will be
and it's not good enough?

Pluck a woman off
the street,
plunge my tongue down
her throat.

Romance a thought,
feel the breeze,
clear the mind,
and it's not good enough.
Happiness is fear.
If I try to ride it, I'll choke.
A rise to a fall,
a cancer to a hope.

What if it's never
as good
as it was when
it wasn't good enough?

CHUBBY LITTLE BIRDS

Chubby little birds,
double-headed women,
hangin' onto verbs,
creep quiet on Fourth Avenue
between the midday sun
and the morning's dew.
A crop of excuses still plagues me
from the gravel on Union Square
to the open skies of Kansas City.
If I travel,
I'll take you with me.

PERFECT HIGH

The perfect weather of early fall and mid spring has been ruined.
All by a perfect high
dating back to 2007 or eight.
I can't remember.
The range of possibilities that cause a window of temperature, just
right.
The science that creates the comfortable amount of shade.
The position of the earth towards the sun.
The courtesy of the wind to know when to blow and when to stand
still.
Fucked up by a small blue pill.

The agonizing smile of a woman
who loved me
has been taken away from me
by a perfect high dating back
to 2015. I can remember
the light of the setting sun
and the incoming night sky on the French Riviera balanced perfectly
off her face.
The Mediterranean gleaning from her eyes and
cosmic conversation
over authentique bouillabaisse,
mostly erased. Turned into a memory of a memory by a small green
pill.

The greatest story ever told has been ruined by an impatient spoiler.
The perfect song impeded by static and you can't find the balance to
rid it.
The drugs, man. The drugs did it.

THERE YOU WERE

There you were.
Here we are.
I can tell your smile is real.
It rips past my eyes,
down the back of my throat.
Rests in my chest
and settles in my stomach.
My legs go hard and numb.
Now I hear you laugh and
I feel myself move through every part
of the city of Boston
and the parts of me left in
Anne Sexton's hometown.
I let it sit with me.
If it stays now, burns now,
it won't later.
Sit outside and smoke a cigarette.
Trust what I've lost and hope.
I'll learn that if I look,
I'll see you still exist
and that's okay.

INVITED

Under the stars so serene,
surrounded by blinking eyes and beating hearts,
a King Rat took his Queen
and before us, a beautiful life starts.

The smoke rises—sparks ignite.
The rain holds—then it falls.
She tells me to dance—I just might.
There are no bounds here—no laws.

To Love, we raise our champagne.
Except for us, that it's caused too much pain.
We witness love united.
I'm just happy I was invited.

ACHE

My stomach hurt.
I was having trouble keeping my eyes open.
 Sitting on the train, pressed up against the cold metal pole,
resting my red,
 beaten face against the metal.
The standing riders attempting to find space to hold on
 while I tried to breathe in
as much of the air conditioning as I could
while enjoying the last moments of the dark tunnel
 before the 4 train spat out into the bright Yankee Stadium
infused outdoors of the Bronx.

SHOULDER BLADES

I don't know your name.
But, aayy.
I know your shoulder blades.
Cascade,
make ya numb
like novocaine.
Parade,
you around my brain.
Same days
so, I know your pain.
Touché on your track, hun.
Tattoos on your back, love.
Please know that I'm back here.
There's a car coming
in my mind,
running.
Maybe one day I'll ask your name.
'Til then...

33

WE ALL DIE SOMETIMES

We all die sometimes.
I hope you are all
high on drugs
because how can you not be?

I felt dirty.
And being done with trying
to justify who I am
left me weightless.

And tied to the ground,
between my ears
felt like a department store's
lost and found.

Keep coming back.
Stay.
I wasn't alone in rehab
on Christmas Day.

I was alone with the door locked,
my brown water stopped working.
My hands kept shaking.
Soon I'll turn fuckin' thirty.

Mickey went back to the bars.
I ask him,
"What did you learn?"
He says,
"Nothing."

WRONG

The reality is
that sometimes
no matter how much you thought
you were right about something
no matter how long you believed it
you were wrong

BAD BANANA

"Yo, man. I'm lookin' for that Kanye West." The voice on the phone sounded nervous.

"Sorry, bro. I'm in the city right now. I should be back around five."

"Umm. Okay. You have it...sorry, him, though?"

"Yea."

"Will you hold three for me?"

"Yea, bro. No problem." Mario was starting to get annoyed with this conversation.

"Like, definitely, though?"

"I said yes, dude. Damn. I'll call you, bro."

"I'll just hit you back up around five. That cool?"

"Whatever, bro." Mario hung up the phone. "Jesus Christ, duuuude. Fuckin' fiends!" He looked over to the passenger seat where Pete sat staring out the window at the East River. They were parked on the corner of Eighty-Fourth and East End Avenue. "You alright, Pete?"

"Yeah, bro. High as fuck. That blunt got me stuck." Pete, known by his boys as Sneaky Pete, and by the girls as Creepy Pete, sat shotgun, his hand down the front of his sweatpants with his winter hat hanging sideways off the side of his head. "Tell me that blunt wasn't mean as fuck? I roll the best Ls. You know it." He turned his chubby, red-eyed face towards Mario and smiled.

"I mean, we had to light it like thirty-three times. But it wasn't too bad."

"Whatever."

Mario checked his phone. One new text: *You got any more of those Kanye Wests?* He didn't answer the text.

Mario was twenty-nine years old and tired. He was tired of dealing with the losers he grew up with in Yonkers. He had wanted out as a kid and for a while there he had gotten out when he was with Kim. Now he was back. The guys who he grew up with and admired were all out, living elsewhere. Or if they were still in Yonkers, they had good jobs and families. There were guys he looked up to who were now dead or in jail. It was a fifty-fifty split. His boys who were left were all similar to Sneaky Pete—out of shape, no ambition, and just wanting to get high all day. Mario was six-foot-two, in good shape, with dark brown eyes and full lips. He was tough-looking, handsome, and quiet. None of his other friends were quiet. They never shut the fuck up.

"I'm just saying, Mo, when J or Tim rolls blunts, they all loose and shit. Weed be fallin' all on yo' tongue and shit." Mario hated how

35

Pete spoke. He had known Pete since he was nine. Pete went to Catholic school. Pete's parents were still married and they had money. It's like he earned the dialect by being a loser. "My blunts, they burn slow and shit, getting us optimal—"

"Yo, shut up. I want to hear this." Mario turned up the radio.

Another case reported today of what people are calling the East Side Slapper. Today, at 1:13 p.m., Officer Lola Martinez was walking on Eighty-Sixth Street and Lexington Avenue with two other officers when a tall, Caucasian male came striding past, striking Officer Martinez in the face. The officers chased the man but were unable to catch him. The man is said to be tall, six-foot-three to six-foot-five, with blond hair and blond eyebrows, and is most likely between the ages of twenty-five and thirty-five. This is the third account of such a crime in the last ten days. The NYPD is asking people to be on the lookout for the man, who has been running around the east side of Manhattan...

"Wow, that's crazy. Dude's just going around slapping cops."

"Crazy. I read about this, shit."

"Crazy. The East Side Bitch Slapper!" Sneaky Pete laughed hard at his own joke.

"I read a headline of an article on Facebook this morning and been thinking about it all day."

"Yo. What's taking this dude so long? I thought he said one o'clock?"

"He did. He'll be here soon. What are you in a hurry to do?" Pete shrugged his shoulders, half agreeing and half making it clear he didn't like waiting. "Yo, why weren't you at Eric's thing the other night? It was actually pretty fun."

"I was sick, bro. Ate a bad banana."

Mario turned his head slowly toward his passenger, his mouth slightly ajar, his eyes open wide."

"You did what?"

"I had food poisoning or some shit. I ate a bad banana."

"Yooooo. That's not a thing bro!" Mario started laughing and shaking his head in disbelief.

"What you mean that's not a thing? It had a bad part. All brown and shit. And I ate that shit anyway. Then I got sick." Pete looked confused.

"Yo, it's not like milk or fuckin' chicken. It's just extra sugar or whatever. That shit doesn't make you sick. Whatever, dude. I'm gonna smoke a cigarette."

Mario got out of the car and stood looking north to where East End Ave meets FDR Drive. He started to think about Kim. He was only with her for six months, but they had been fucking around while she was still married and while he was still with his old girl. He had been crazy about her. So when she left her husband and they got their own place in Jersey, it had been the happiest six months of his life. He still didn't understand what happened, why she went back. He played it off to his boys like it was no big thing, just another bitch. But for those six months, he was happy. He was out of Yonkers. He even enjoyed when her daughter would come over every other weekend. He couldn't admit to guys like Creepy Pete how much it hurt. She hadn't reached out one time. Not once in nine months. Why? He had to delete her number so he would stop calling her. He remembered the area code was 913, but luckily, he hadn't memorized the rest.

He flicked his cigarette and began to get back in the car. Sneaky Pete was crushing up a pill on a CD case and jerked at the sound of the door. He tried to hide it, but it was too late.   "Dude! What the fuck! I told you..."

"I'm sooorrry, dude. I thought you would take longer smoking that cig, bro. Smoked that shit mad fast and shit."

"So? What the fuck, Pete? That doesn't make it better. You told me you didn't bring any. We are out here waiting to cop, the car probably reeks of bud, and here you are crushin' up oxys in the fuckin' passenger seat? Fuck you, man." Mario took the half of his body that was leaning into the car out and slammed the door. Through the closed window he heard a muffled, "I'm soooorrry, brooo."

Then Pete blew the line that was on the CD case and sat with his head down, pressing his thumb over his right nostril and inhaling hard with his left, getting everything down. Mario walked half a block away from the car, furious. He lit another cigarette and thought, *Why do I hang out with these fuckin' losers?*

Whenever he didn't like the situation he found himself in, his anger from one issue would transfer into another. A small annoyance would turn into a big picture disappointment. He couldn't help it. He would start to think about when his life was good. When he was away from these morons and when he was working a real job and had a real existence to go home to—when he was with Kim. These thoughts would drive him further into a rage and when he got like this, he knew his temper could easily flare out of control. He was known to lash out. He looked at his phone: 1:42. His guy had him waiting forty minutes and had told him he was running only ten minutes late. Later tonight, Mario would be playing that same game with people up in Yonkers, but at least he wasn't withdrawing while he waited like those fiends would be. He felt a tantrum coming on.

Then he saw something coming down the avenue. He nearly dropped his cigarette. It was a tall, thin, blond man running in elegant full strides down East End towards him. It reminded him of something you see on the Discovery Channel, like footage of a gazelle. His strides were hypnotizing, and Mario caught himself frozen as he watched the man come closer and closer. It all happened so fast. As the man passed, he turned his head and his bright blue eyes pierced through Mario's chest. He didn't slow down, but he gave him a quick wink and kept going, making an abrupt ninety-degree turn left onto Eighty-Fifth Street.

Mario swiftly walked towards his car and got into the driver's seat.

"Yo, man. You ain't gonna be all salty towards me all day now, are you? I know how you get. I only brought half a pill, man. Half a thirty. It wasn't even a Kanye, bro. I thought this would take mad faster bro, but—"

"Shut up, Pete. You are not going to believe what I just saw."

"What's up?" Mario shook his head and smiled.

"Remember the radio? Dude, I just—" At that moment, his phone vibrated in his pocket. "Yo, this is probably our guy now. Hold up." He fished his phone out of his deep pocket. "You're not going to believe this when I tell you." He pulled his phone out and saw an unsaved number was calling him. The first three digits were 913, and right when he read the next seven, he remembered Kim's number. Mario's heart began to beat so hard he thought he would be physically sore afterward. His hands went clammy and it was suddenly hard to grip the phone. Pete asked him who it was, but his throat was numb like he forgot how to talk. Time slowed down. He forgot where he was. He answered. It took effort to mutter out a croaky, "Hello." There were a few seconds of dead air and he could hear her breathing on the other end.

"Mario...it's me. It's Kim."

"I know." He tried to hide any tone in his voice that would indicate he'd been waiting for this, any desperation. "What's up, Kim? How are you?"

"Listen, I know this is kind of awkward to call you about, and I feel bad about it, but do you have any...I was told to call it Kanye West?"

LOTTERY TICKETS

Lottery tickets
Time keepers
Yo
the train's here

All these words
left
to type into my notepad
I'll take the local
breathe in the fresh carbon
that is the morning R train

I think I'm tired of being in a hurry
I'm not getting anywhere anyway
I have a couple different books
on me
Pop-Tarts
Coffee and a banana
I think I'll write a silly poem
about dogs today
I listen to my BBC News podcast
News flash
Donald Trump's
a fuckin' punk ass

I can't figure out why
my bedroom's so hot
I turned the heat off
I pulled my sheets off
I'm reminded of all
the unsolved murders

Today
take me away from me
I'm out to get me
What's the difference between
the night sky and a black eye
If I had three wishes
I'd ask twice to be open-minded
and then to mind my own business

39

FLY WITH ME

You were a prisoner
of my anxiety
and I asked you
to fly with me

You were a deity
displayed on the street
with my vanity
You were my piece of meat

Rise and fall with me
We'll turn two to three
I'll take all that's free
Take away anything that you could be

Was it too much to ask
to give up your life
kill your dreams
and be my wife

TRUST

A cocaine-induced psychosis
mixed with an
"I'll hurt anyone once"
diagnosis.
Trailing behind the rest of my peers.
—Maturity in low doses.
I can't keep my thoughts straight
and they know this.
Every good thing I've tried,
I've lost focus.
Any day now and I'll
be with the roses.

TOO LONG SHARE

Her smile made me want to be quiet.
And on top of that,
she,
all in green and pink and black,
was shorter than I
expected.

You can't sit anywhere in this town.
And if you rest your
breath,
all it seems we think
is tested.

More and more, now I'm calm
and less angry.
What does it mean to move?
Travel back and forth to the
same beds.
Made or intimidated mazes.
Less intimidated phases.
I am
more or less willing to live
outside my cages.

Her eyes made me want to share her
with a stranger.
Life's flavored fairness
left me careless.
Green and pink and black.
A sudden serenity attack.

THERE IS POETRY IN THIS

"There is poetry in this,"
he says about his own condition,
coming to terms with who
he is
and his pointless mission.
He takes a page from the ghosts,
admits it's just death
with a brief intermission.
A life of flowing water
to a solitary prison.
Tales of broken men
and rising spirits.
Annihilated glory
and awkward sex positions.
Clocks with minds of their
own.
Hopeless souls stripped to the bone.

The last image he sees
is day through the
fallen curtains,
pushed away by swollen knuckles
clenched in a tired fist.
He says to himself using just breath,
"There is poetry in this."

PORTRAIT

A friend once told me that if you eat spicy food right before you go to sleep you'll have nightmares. I had been trying it out for a few nights but didn't see a pattern. I still dreamt about her. I still woke up in shock from what my life had become. I welcomed nightmares. I welcomed the moment when I realized it they weren't real—that shock back to life, the deflation from my chest. Unlike the dreams where she was lying next to me, where I would seize up upon coming to, remembering she wasn't there. In this instant, I woke up and it wasn't morning and I hadn't been dreaming of anything. The darkness reminded me I was at my father's house in the country.

I started experiencing these moments about six months into being sober again. I would only get them in the middle of the night, usually when waking up needing to use the bathroom, still half asleep. They are easy to describe but impossible to explain. It's as simple as—I am me. I exist. I am who I am. I am here. This is my name. These moments would come to me fully, all at once, and I would instantly become overwhelmed. But as quickly as they came, they left and I would drift back to sleep. This particular night I had a moment before getting out of bed to use the bathroom. I lay in the black room, eyes unadjusted and came to believe that I was who they said I was, a human being with a certain name, who has done certain things. Then I got up to pee.

When I passed the mirror, I noticed. I thought about it while I peed and then passed the mirror again. And I saw it again. I almost made it into the hallway when I decided to turn back to get a better look. I turned on the light and there he was. He had to be in his eighties. It took me a few seconds to come to terms with what I was looking at. It was me, but old. He wasn't so much a reflection as a separate person looking back at me. He didn't seem afraid.

I saw his watery eyes and white hair, the lines in his face and the yellow on his teeth. None of it bothered me much. He looked frail but otherwise healthy. I was alarmed by the muscles around his shoulders and neck. They were loose. Despite that, he looked vigorous. I felt comfortable looking him up and down. He did the same to me. We were curious about each other.

I saw life and loss in him. I saw people I missed. I saw people who came into my life as plain and insignificant who then became unique and painfully one of a kind. I felt the panic of them leaving me and how they could never be replaced. I indirectly witnessed how their passivity turned to confidence. Quiet turned to humility. Cynicism to wit. Some of the hardest things I have faced, and still have to face, have been and will be brought on by letting certain people in. His eyes told me some things are better left alone. They just didn't say what.

Looking at him, I remembered the advice I had been given as a teenager— it's better to regret something you did than something you didn't do. I would live by this mantra most my life, but would not pass it on to others. I saw how much pain it caused. I followed it, not sure if I believed it.

This was not some vision into the future or some discovery of myself as an old man. It wasn't a reflection of my life or an opportunity to see my mistakes. Here I was, observing myself at a different age. I watched as he did the same to me, silently looking me up and down. If I looked back into his eyes, I could feel his losses, and also triumphs. There were no visions and nothing had to be said. I could read these attributes on his face. I could tell by the way he carried the weight in his shoulders where his stress had been.

I saw philosophy. I learned by looking at him that in each and every person there is a pulsating philosophy— billions of temporary sets of unique vessels walking around, killing time, and making noise. I saw conflict. He had his set of principles and what drove him, as did I. Neither of us believed most of them, and that was visible to me. With that, I felt anger towards him along with a sense of hypocrisy. I had begun to see the qualities of myself that I didn't respect existing in him.

"Let's be brave," I said under my breath. I wanted to walk away. I had a sneaky suspicion he didn't want to be here either. Was he scared? He had to have more courage than I did, right? Time must have made him stronger than I was standing there. Or had he become weaker? Would I become weaker as I grew older? My best friend lost his girlfriend a few years before that night. After years of grieving, reflecting, and coping, he came to the conclusion that whatever doesn't kill you doesn't always make you stronger. You can get weaker throughout your life. Obstacles can break you and you can live on, no stronger from them.

The old man didn't look like my father. But then again, neither did I. Around the time of this night, I had been struggling with the idea that maybe he wasn't my father. My mother had been unfaithful consistently throughout her relationship with him. I never got any tests done to find out. I didn't ever bring it up to him. My father was my father and he always would be. He wasn't perfect, but he was mine. On the drive from the city to his house, we had a conversation about what we found most important to us. He gave an answer I had heard many times before—the collecting of memories. Through traveling— eating, drinking, and experiencing new cultures—my father had been collecting memories his entire life. He was proud of that. He had traveled all over the world, and he could sit down on the couch at the end of the night, pour himself a glass of red wine, and revisit these places.

I had agreed with my father's answer for years, albeit I was far less traveled than he was. But since the breakup, I found it hard to look back on the places I had been with my ex without feeling the pain of loss I associated with her. On top of that, I started to see a pattern in the way I looked at traveling. There was always a strong companionship associated with the most recent place I had been, whether it was a great experience or not. Past adventures seemed to get watered down by the newer ones. I was learning that memories fade. And anything that fades cannot be the most important thing in life. Memories die with you. They are only as vital as you are. How important can one imagine he is, to think the most meaningful thing in life is only as big as himself?

My answer was art. Any form. Anything manmade that stands separate from the man himself. The capacity to make something, bringing them into a reality that is bigger than just existing. Maybe at that point in my life I simply had to believe that there was something bigger than me.

Looking at another version of myself was not unfamiliar. I had had this bad habit my entire life. As early as junior high I was obsessed with looking in on myself from a theoretical, different perspective, like a viewer watching a show. Did this old man still do that? Was he doing that right now? He did come to me. I felt a wave of disappointment run through me and I turned off the bathroom light.

When I crawled back into bed, I thought about when I was a child. The most frightening thing was being the last one in the house awake. As an adult, I had trouble going to bed if anyone else was still up. It would be a long time before I had another moment.

ELEGANTLY POOR

We,
so elegantly poor,
lay half asleep in my bed.
I
wait for you to come back through the door.

Half awake,
I taste
the middle of your back.
We
met in the tail end of a panic attack.

I'll wait
impatiently while your phone breaks
apart—surprised how hard your bad day affected
me.

That you set me free would be a lie.
Your half smile and loose glasses,
with a quick look back up the stairs.
A broken year as jilted lovers.
We agree we deserve each other.

I FEEL LIKE A HUMAN BEING

I feel like a human being,
not like a thought or an idea.
People swarming around me like
a keepsake tornado.
For the first time, a bag of bones
with a soul.
Not a concept
or a war treaty.
A beast with shoulders and feet,
not a fleeting feeling.
I'll stay awake until I go to sleep.
I've just accepted I have a heart
that's beating.

VOTE

For a moment,
no light shines through.
And we can discuss whether or not
casual sex sounds fun for you.

Ripped apart between
what's new and what makes me
feel sick,
is another challenge waiting to begin.

A free—at least cheap—motion.
A hand shaking,
carrying a gun.
You take a moment to apply the lotion.

I feel me beginning to take part
in activities that will send me too far.
A creep stalking in the dark.
Another lonely drug addict
trying to make it right.

So, let's put me to a vote.
Should I be allowed
to wait in the back row
while you decide if these thoughts
were born into day or night?

You say, "Don't you believe in democracy?"
I say, "Sweetheart, I believe in everything."

STEPS

When I see her writing
on these steps,
I think of the thoughts
in other people's brains.

We come. We came,
not one in the same
But routinely alike,
we all still feel pain.

I read the list wrong,
or it was old.
Either way, it was off.
Where you were once warm, you are now cold.

I guess I love this city,
but your guess is as good as mine.
It's too fast and the weather's shitty,
but on these steps, I'll pass some time.

ALONE

She sits next to me.
I shake with her.
Unmistakable breaks occur.
She's come and gone,
fleeing breath and wakes and nerves.
I ask her to leave but now she rapes
her turn.
I ask for loneliness to shake and now I'm stuck with her.
Before she died, she filled me in taxidermy.
An evil bitch, she sticks around and says,
"If you want to leave me, kill yourself and do it to my face."

GOD

To me, God is everything.
It's the strangers on the train,
the smell of my saliva on her tits.
It's the times I told them they were stupid for saying it exists.

The wonder
of the gap between her legs.
The way my smoke tastes in the morning.
It's why I'm still here. Still going.

Rilke taught me who God is.
Leonard Cohen seconded his opinion.
Alan Watts explained what it's not,
and everything it's got.

God helps me be free.
It doesn't have a gender.
It doesn't have a look.
It's got nothing and it's got nothing
to prove.
At least not to me.

CODEPENDENTLY ADDICTED

Would my words exist if you were
not there to read them?
Would my mind create new thoughts
if you were not there to believe them?

I think I got too worried
when you didn't answer your phone.
I'd like to think I wouldn't still
be tripped up or
feel buried by
the thought of being left alone.

A constant grip of letting go.
Now I just want to rest,
home alone,
across too many miles for me to
ever know.
Codependently addicted to
what, in two words, we'll call
solitude,
fear.

I pack my bags and put them on the floor.
A lucid need to feel empty
from a forgettable life
to a glamorous cemetery.

"You are doing just fine." And I'd agree,
then stare off, off the East Coast,
and remember a time when life didn't
hurt so much.

When I could still get high.

THE PARISHIONER

In March, he ascended from the church basement realizing there was no world for him in there. But when he got to the front steps, he froze, remembering there was no more world for him out there either. The Long Island Railroad was only a block away and he wanted to hop on and head back into the city. To what? There was no more apartment, his girl had left, and his job was gone. So he was stuck on the front steps of this curious, small church.

When his father moved to Long Island from Manhattan five years earlier, one of the first things he noticed was this church. The neighborhood was made up entirely of neatly formed rows of houses in every direction bordered by two active railroad tracks for the commuters about two miles apart. The only exception was this single steeple church that sat on the corner of one of these streets, the only non-domestic structure. His father's house was located parallel to the church and one street east, and he could see the steeple from the guest bedroom window, which as of this morning when he was released, would be his bedroom window.

His heart raced while he took shallow breaths, trying to figure out where he belonged. His father was home cooking dinner and his fifteen-year-old brother, fifteen years his junior, was probably starting his homework. His friends were probably at a happy hour or still at work or beginning to start their shifts at the bars. The other patients he woke up with this morning were finishing up group, probably arguing about the dinner line. And where was his girl? It had been two months since she left him, and that question weighed on his mind almost all the time. Where could he go? Back into the church basement was out of the question, yet stepping off the front steps was proving to be too terrifying.

He was suspended on those steps for only a few minutes, but it felt much longer. Then it passed. It passed because that's what happens with feelings, they come and then they go. He didn't know that at the time, and that might have been the first time he really let himself experience it. He walked the block to his father's driveway and sat on the cool pavement. Looking towards the church steeple, he tried to cry but nothing happened.

By June, with a clear head, the future progressed slow enough for him to evaluate the daily workings of the budding leaves. In the meantime, he began to find a world for himself both in and outside of the church. With little alternative, he decided to stay at his father's

51

for a few months. He got a low-paying job in the city and commuted in daily. Three nights a week he ventured down into the church's basement. It took some time before he could sleep at night, but that too began to happen. He would find himself throughout the day fluctuating between anger and joy in great waves. It seemed the angry moments lasted longer.

His greatest friends were his father's two dogs: two West Highland Terriers named Rukus and Harold. He would take them on long walks around the neighborhood, often getting lost because he couldn't distinguish one street from the other. The church's steeple was the only marker to help him place where he was. Since March, he had had some of his lowest moments on the axis of the suburban grids. On these walks, he would allow himself to feel. He would stop at a corner and look around, wondering what he was doing there, how he got there. He would grow angry over the weather or the way the leashes would tangle together. He would curse out loud and throw tantrums. He would think of all he lost and he would well up in tears. On other walks, he would notice the beautiful purples and oranges of the sunset. With Spring fully bloomed, he would breathe in all the smells and have these fleeting moments of calm and gratitude. They were much shorter, but often more powerful than his fits of sadness and rage. Back at his father's and during his workday, he would do his best to suppress the pain. His body would fill up with heat and he would start to feel his heartbeat against his ribs. The dread and anxiety would come to a pinnacle like he was going to explode, but he would then slowly digress into melancholy.

One afternoon, he was sitting at home feeling sorry for himself. He was trying to explain to Rukus that it was raining too hard to go outside, but Rukus was still giving him the "let's go" face. He suited up and hooked the anxious pups to their leashes, ignoring his stepmother's rule to use the harness for Harold, and headed out into the rain. He planned for a short walk, just around the church and back. When he got to the church, his step-mother's rule proved worthy when Harold saw a squirrel and took off, sliding out of his collar. Harold ran towards the back of the church and he chased after him, dragging the more complacent Rukus behind him.

Harold was sniffing and exploring in the backyard of the little church, having lost the squirrel. The garden, in the backyard of the church, was hidden from the street. It was rectangular-shaped and guarded by a thin rope. There were tomatoes and peppers and all sorts of vegetables growing. He had never been behind the church before. Harold was inside the ropes sniffing around and he shouted angrily in whispers for him to come over. After a few calls, the dog came back and when Harold approached him he rolled over on his back, admitting his guilt. He hooked him back up to the collar and looked at the back of the church. The front had clearly been renovated more recently than the back and he observed all the old crumbling stone windowsills and the decrepit wooden back door. He wondered how old the church was and why they had not finished renovations to the back. He walked around the circumference of the garden one full time and then headed home.

When he got into his father's foyer, he did his best to dry the dogs with a towel before they started sprinting around the house and drying their bodies on the carpet. He knew what he was going to do next, but he couldn't explain why. He also couldn't stop himself or slow himself down. His heartbeat was in his throat as he walked over and grabbed the house phone off the hook. Even though he had been with her for so many years, he didn't have the number memorized. So he took out his cell and opened the contact. Pushing the numbers made him feel like a kid again. He stood anxiously as it rang. When he heard her voice on the other end, he wasn't able to speak. He exhaled hard and cleared his throat. "When you were with me, did you feel like you stopped learning?"

She gave her answer, sort of. It was more like she pleaded confusion at the question. She quickly merged to wondering about him and what was happening. Even though he didn't receive a yes or no, he got the answer needed and hung up on her mid-sentence.

He remembered in September how they told him he would feel his feelings. So he suited up every day ready for a battle against himself. The world seemed big and life passed quickly, but his reality was small and felt slow. He had a routine, something he swore he would never do. He also, for years, swore he wouldn't put a needle in his arm or drink in the morning, so maybe he was done with swearing. Three nights a week he would venture back down into that church basement and the other nights he would explore others. He didn't like his job, but he enjoyed how little stress there was. The money was awful, and it required a great deal of humility. He spent too many minutes on the clock thinking about what his friends were doing with their lives and their careers as he moved boxes seemingly from one spot to another to collect dust. It was a limbo period between his previous life and the future.

The future did exist. It sat at the reception desk in the offices of the warehouse. It had green eyes and skin the color of espresso with a splash of milk and a 1970s pixie haircut. It spoke with an accent and its teeth shone like the snow on the sunny day after a blizzard. It was nice to him, even though in his eyes he was not worth even the morning hellos.

Be kind to yourself.

The group in the church basements would tell him things like this.

Let it go. Give it away. Be kind and respectful. If it's meant to be it will be.

And shit like that.

But he did exactly that, and by the week of his birthday, they were out having coffee for the second time. He remembered from being a kid, before liquid courage, that in order to make a girl comfortable, you needed to establish a few inside jokes. These first bouts of recurring jokes are always awful and rightfully fade away after the first few weeks.

He kissed her. She kissed him back. He wondered what type of girl she was. She knew he spent evenings in church basements, and she told him that it was admirable. "I'm proud of you," she said. He thought about how she didn't even know him.

He stayed over. The second time was better. In bed, she told him that she would love to meet these dogs he talked so much about. She grew up in Pakistan and her father never let them have a dog. Since she got here six years ago, she always volunteered to walk her friends' dogs or dog sit if she could. He invited her over for dinner.

His stepmother told them shortly after she arrived that they would be having dinner in the dining room and not in the kitchen like they usually did. This made him uneasy. He didn't want to scare her. He was especially nervous about his teenage brother being there. This seemed like a situation that he should be in. A girl coming over to his parents' house, the house he lives in, to eat dinner—like his dad should drive the girl home while he started in on his homework.

At one point during the meal, his brother took attention away from the mild interviewing by telling a fabricated account of being offered weed at a Burger King.

"Ya know," his father began. "I have half a mind to go down to the police station and tell them this. It's not right." His stepmother made eye contact with the rest of the table while rolling her eyes.

"Dad! Don't. Please!" came from his brother, wishing he had not said anything, mostly because it probably wasn't true. He smiled at his guest and also rolled his eyes. She smiled back and fluttered her eyelashes and tilted her head to the side, showing him that she found all this cute.

"It's not right," his father continued. "I have a few things I want to tell these cops. The dog at the end of the block? Huh? That dog is vicious! There are kids on this block. Just a matter of time, really." He took a bite of food and they all thought it was over. "But the thing that I really want to talk to them about is the parking on the side of the church there." He gestured with his fork out the window, pointing at the steeple that was currently in front of a full moon making it look like a pizza pie missing a slice. "The people...what do you call them?" He looked at his wife but didn't give her enough time to answer. "The way they park on Sundays." He turned and now looked at their guest, knowing the rest of the family had heard this rant. "The parking lots on the sides fill up, right? Then the people, they park on the side, on the street. They park sideways, sticking out. It's not right. It's dangerous. There is going to be an accident." The guest nodded in passionate agreement, mouth full of food. "And the cops do nothing! No tickets. Nothing. And why? Because they are..."

"Parishioners," his stepmother said while touching his arm and giving him a look the family knew to mean, *Calm Down. We have company.* His father nodded and took a breath and smiled.

"Yeah. Parishioners. Still, it's not right. They should at least get tickets like everybody else," he said, forcing a smile.

Come January, it had been a year since his fiancée left him. In that year, he learned that emotional withdrawals are similar to withdrawals from heroin. The horrors. Punching in a dream. There were nights, once he let himself start feeling, where he would lay awake tossing and turning, sweating, on the verge of panic, but in the morning, it would be less. Each time he sweat it out, so to speak, it was less, and less again.

When his new friend started to become distant, he assumed it was him. She was calling less and was less available to hang out. She would stop responding in the middle of text conversations and he would wait, pacing around his room, the guest room, preparing for the worst. She was moving on from him. Him, living with his parents, unable to meet at the bar. He would ask what was wrong when he would catch her staring off into her own world, and she would assure him it was nothing.

When she told him she had to talk to him, he was already steps ahead. How would he find another girl? He had been lucky to find one in his present situation. Who else would want a guy like him?

"My father is ill. He isn't getting better. It's all happened very quickly, but I am leaving on Thursday for Karachi." Thursday was two days away. Karachi was in Pakistan.

"I am so sorry," he said, hugging her even though she gave a small amount of pushback. "It's good you are going. I am sure he will be very happy to see you." It took every sensible thought in his being not to ask how long she would be gone, knowing it would take as long as it took. She mentioned that he didn't have long for the world, which left him sad for her but optimistic she wouldn't be gone too long.

She left a few days after the new year. She was there less than two days when they pronounced her father dead. The arrangements for a proper Muslim funeral took a few days and in all this time, he heard from her once when she told him he had passed. Every day he waited for her to contact him and let him know when she would be returning.

The month went by slowly. His family was driving him crazy. He was coming up on his thirty-first birthday. The idea of finding his own place left him feeling anxious and frustrated and each time he looked into it, he felt further away from it. He had successfully spoiled the dogs and now they were constantly demanding him to feed them or take them out and he never had the heart to turn them down. His job was becoming more and more mundane by the hour and the process of looking for another was similar to looking for housing. He had learned the hard way in the past not to put his happiness in the hands of a woman, but if he was honest with himself, his friend returning was the only thing he felt would cheer him up.

So when she called him on a Wednesday and told him that she would be returning on the upcoming Sunday, all the problems he was facing seemed manageable. He went on Craigslist and looked at a few different rooms and called their owners. He asked his stepmother for a loan and even picked apart his résumé and applied online to a few different jobs. It was the most productive four days since he had checked himself out of the hospital ten months earlier. He didn't let her know he was doing any of this and planned to tell her when she returned. He was going to ask her to be his girlfriend, officially. But going forward, he would have his own place and a new invigoration. She was the one he wanted to be with. He was ready to start his new life. He wanted to start it with her.

When she called him the day before she was set to return, he answered his phone joyously and went to dive right into the plans he had made for the following night. She stopped him before he got the first giddy word out of his mouth.

"I violated my visa." The words rang in his ear. Over the next few minutes, he bargained with her, with the situation, and then grew frustrated with how calmly she was taking it. She knew there was no sense in fighting. She knew that it wasn't a fight and that she wasn't coming back, not anytime soon. After only a few minutes, she grew tired of his struggle and hung up the phone. He was mid-sentence.

He walked past the dogs laying on the kitchen floor. They popped up thinking it was time to go outside. He put on his hat and his coat and walked out the side door leaving them behind. His heart was beating and his thighs were heavy. He didn't know where he was going, but he was moving forward, toward the church. There were no cars in the parking lot and no cars sticking out onto the street. He entered the church through the side entrance. There was no one inside. He walked into the chapel and tried to sit down, but his body wouldn't let him. He walked out of the chapel and into the back rooms of the empty Sunday School, pacing. There were student projects pinned on to the bulletin boards up and down the hall.

His breathing was shallow and he started to get light-headed. He forced himself to stop and he put both hands against a wall, closed his eyes, and rested his forehead against the cool plaster. He started to control his breathing, taking long deep breaths until he didn't feel so panicked.

When he was able to open and focus his eyes, he was staring at a wall that had about twelve student coloring projects pinned up. They were all the same coloring sheet with their unique coloring jobs. The outline was a blank rainbow, with blank clouds surrounding it, and under the arch of the rainbow in bold text it read, *I can trust in God because.* Each student had created their own scheme in crayon. Some were your typical rainbow, others had personalized patterns, and some students had drawn little stars or hearts inside the lines of the structure. His eyes panned the pictures up and down until the one in the bottom row, all the way in the right corner caught his eye. There were the outlines of the rainbow, the outline of the clouds, and the words. *I can trust in God because.* This particular student had decided not to color within the lines at all. Instead, there were violent lines erratically scribbled across the entire page, as if the student picked up a fist of random crayons and scratched his or her interpretation of chaos, the outermost spasm, in black.

Slowly, so not to rip the edges at all, he peeled the tape off. He folded up the child's picture and put it inside his front coat pocket. He walked out the front exit and stopped on the steps. He looked back into the church, then forward toward the railroad tracks that headed back into the city.

NEEDS AND WANTS

In here
sometimes I feel alone
looking for instant satisfaction
from my phone
Making a skinny white girl
and the unknown
my future bride
my burden to hold
She sleeps on a bed with
her friend
while I picture us walking
on the Hudson
The breeze from another borough
a Band-Aid in another hurry
I'll lose all of my attention
for a pretty smile
and a fixed erection
Make up the bad with the good
Overthink it like only
I
know how
Creating images of split blistered innocence
I need what I don't want
I count the water in the river
and pray I'll be happy never

A LITTLE COMMUTE

I want to live in a town where I can
see the trees over the rooftops.
Where I can create problems
instead of solutions to solve them.

A circus car on a highway.
Ladies and gentlemen with
umbrellas and iPhones hellbent on
blocking my way home.

It's lonely and crowded.
I'm knocked out but
still conscious.
I take a breath—it tastes obnoxious.

I'm older now
and the only difference is,
the music in my headphones
is safer.

New York continues to be the
woman
who makes me smell
but forbids to taste her.

A WOMAN COLLAPSES

A woman collapses.
I see your red face
in hers.
Your sad face.
The one you make when
you're sick or
feel disgrace.
Before you cry.
The face you had on when
you said goodbye.

That face
brings me to a place
where I believe
I'll never replace
the concern,
the passion
I gave.
That maybe letting you go,
forcing you out,
was my biggest
mistake.

SOMEONE ELSE

So now she's probably off with
someone else
and you're stuck inside your cage of hell.
I guess only time will tell.

If you'll get out and walk again.

How could she exist
outside of the web you twist?
Summer skin, a morning kiss.
Her eyes are now on his.

But life goes on for you.
Be a man—see it through.
While she's off with someone else,
you could always go off to Paris and
drink yourself to death.

HENRY

I have always been lost into women,
but now I sleep with a man.
And he cares for me more
than the whole previous clan.

He's been there
through the hardest time of my life.
Now I question
if I'll ever need a wife.

When he sees my pain,
he lays with me all night,
even when I'm acting insane.
When I get home from work,
he gets out of bed.
And when we hug,
I forget all my dread.

I know it's late, but let's go on a walk.
I don't mind that you can't talk.
Anyway, I'm tired of all the noise.
Oh, Henry, you are a good boy.

OUTLINES

I tend to be better equipped
to handle calamities
over minor issues.
When things fall apart,
the world slows down
and I see things more clearly.
I can see the beautiful outlines.

LAST DATE

The light was on.
The door was locked.
She never thought
he would have knocked.

They were in love
in a way she'd never reach.
She was relaxed.
He brought the bleach.

He had not called in weeks.
She could finally sleep.
Even before tonight, he'd done enough.
He was in too deep.

Why she left, she couldn't say.
It wasn't getting better.
Not soon.
Not ever.

He couldn't accept this.
Love was love.
Even knowing why, he came.
He looked forward to one last kiss.

Right when she opened the door,
she knew it was over.
From the look in his eyes,
she knew she would not leave alive.

TRUST THE WATER

In a rush of tactile symmetry,
he heard her voice so vividly.
She whispered softly

"You can't get rid of me.
If you can't beat 'em,
you are left to set 'em free.
Teach patience.
Practice chivalry.
You've cornered a beast,
now act accordingly."

I've sobered up long enough to see the moon
and half the plagues that were
drowning you.
I only wish you could see them too.

Alone in a room with nine million people
gazing through the rain at a
pointless steeple.
I realized nothing, all at once.
Except—trust the water and
 you are evil.

YOU ARE EVERYONE

You are everyone
for a split second.
Your face on their bodies
calmly walking towards me.

Your sight surrounds me,
dancing in patterns,
approaching me quickly.
Can't tell what you're after.

Then they turn into strangers.
I don't get to get you.
I feel relieved
and also let down.

If it ever was you
out of nine million of you,
my knees weak, my heart beats.
I lose all my air.

I hope that I never
come in contact
or better,
that you become no one.

THE BODIES

The bodies,
moving forward with their eyes
on the papers.
Narrowly afraid of eviction
from the land of the free,
the home of the scared.

Angry texts to my spouse.
Apologetic pleas to my boss
concerning the delays
on the yellow line.
My news app tells me of
our leader's convictions
and his yellow spine.

Take the Arab's business,
the Mexicans their fruit.
Take the sand from the beach,
the water from the well.
Take the drums from the songs,
the laces from the boots.
Take caramel from the candy,
the dogs from their families.
Take the feeling from our first kisses,
the mystery of the new day.

Just know you'll never take the
direction of the passengers
on New York's subways
who don't need and
will encourage you
to keep your fear.

PEACE SIGN EMOJI

He sends a peace sign emoji.
And that's cool.

I tool around
the underground.
Morning dreaming
of manipulating.
What are seeming to be
good-hearted girls
on their way to school.

After classes,
we'd walk around her campus.
I'd be holding
to keep the good times rolling.
Just keep the good times rolling.
My life starts buckling and folding.
I feel the good times rolling.
But where is she going?
Where is she going?

I send him a peace sign emoji.
He says to himself,
"What a cool guy."

DEAD DRUNKEN HEROES

How much would Hemingway and Raymond Carver
Bukowski
and Oscar Wilde
scoff at my sobriety?
"You gave in and gave up at twenty-eight?"
The words I'd then write
for these old dead white guys
about wanting to get better,
about trying to be sober,
about working a program.
C'mon, man...

In my defense,
they didn't have oxycontin
or Xanax.
But
they also didn't have central air
or autocorrect.

So for my old, white,
dead drunken heroes
who most likely
wouldn't like me,
I'll hold my white privilege close
to my heart.
At my core, I'll be angry with
women.
I won't look to Jesus
to be forgiven.
Most importantly,
I'll hold onto the truth
that statistically
I'll end up drinking
myself to death
at fifty.

DISTANCE

I still feel a phantom twitch in my thumb sometimes. I still feel the colors in my head, but I can't see them. They come back to me in flashes between falling asleep and dreaming. Of all the addictions I've subdued, all the pains I've shaken, not one gets my heart as wild and my shoulders as stiff as the memory of Distance. I take a long breath before I unlock the front door of the bar. It's Tuesday afternoon and I haven't been visited by Les in months. I'm overdue.

I walk in and am wafted by the smell of stale beer. The Whole in the Wall—an old dive with a wooden bar and a matching floor that have each been touched up but not replaced over the past nineteen years, resulting in spotty, discolored wooden patterns. The walls are plastered with old promotional beer and liquor signs that were popular in the nineties—Beck's, Goldschlager, LaBatt Blue—none of which are sold at the Whole in the Wall. The stools are wobbly, the bathrooms are repulsive, and no matter how hard I try and clean it, the place is sticky. There is no kitchen and the popcorn machine hasn't worked in years. But the nine TVs are top of the line and are placed around the big room perfectly so that no matter where you stand on a football Sunday, you can catch all the action by just swiveling your head. Most importantly, booze is cheap here.

I open a bottle of cider I put in the ice machine the night before. I pour a whiskey, swig it back, and chase it out with a cold mouthful of cider. All the TVs are off besides the one in the far corner. It's playing a highlight reel of my favorite football team's game on Sunday and I walk over knowing I shut off all nine before I left last night. I stand directly under the mounted screen and watch the last thirty seconds of the highlight. The moment the schedule for the remainder of the season flashes before my eyes, the TV shuts off. He's watching. *Welcome back, Les.* I don't bother to look around or look outside. I don't stare at each screen or the computer wondering where he's watching from. I stopped caring where he observes from long ago. Acceptance. I finish setting up the bar. I hope to myself out loud that it's not busy tonight. My stress of past due bills isn't worth having to deal with crowds. I used to look forward to a busy bar. It meant money and usually a good time. Now my wish is to get through a slow shift and go home without losing my temper on somebody for asking me through the tap handles what beer we have on tap.

My first bartending gig, the place I met Les, was a busy bar. Cal's—a gourmet burger and craft beer bar during the week that on weekend nights would move the tables, switch from classic rock to top forty, and welcome a long line of Columbia University students. "Club Cal's" would be born for a few hours each night, Thursday through Saturday.

I remember the night well. The owner came up to me before my shift and told me that Kappa was having a pledge night. Once the kids got past the bouncer, they were good to drink and not to worry about IDs. I had met Les once before this night—he had come in and ordered a beer off me on a weekday afternoon and as I was telling him his fake ID was shit, Jon, the other bartender, pulled me aside and told me that he had let the ID slide the afternoon before and the kid gave him a seventy-dollar tip. So I did the same and got the same results. The kid was getting a thrill out of drinking around the happy hour crowd, from drinking alone with other strangers like a grown up. He dressed in a suit and talked like he'd been around. As obnoxious as he was, his tip left a positive impression on me. So I was disappointed, but not at all too surprised when I saw he was pledging for Kappa, the most self-important, well-funded frat on an already self-important, well-funded campus.

He shuffled in with a group of other red-faced freshman along with a few familiar faces from the frat. These pledges had been fed shots back at the dorms with the objective of bringing them out to see who would ring up the highest tabs for the brothers while they study who will make the biggest asses of themselves. Les ordered a round of shots and a round of vodka cranberries for his potential brothers and their girlfriends. He handed me his credit card and made a big to-do about slipping me a hundred-dollar bill with it. A part of me wanted to tell him to go fuck himself on principle, but the coke in my wallet along with the oxycontin for after last call wasn't cheap, so I graciously took it and let him wait less time than the others for refills.

It happened subtly, and it didn't take much. At one point, between the biggest rush of the night and last call, after being embarrassed by an older girl who shot down an advance, I saw something I hadn't expected to see. I saw Les' eyes well up with tears. I had just broken up a quarter of an oxy and mixed it in with a line of coke in the employee bathroom and was feeling sympathetic, which was probably why I didn't just sit back and watch the show. I grabbed him by the arm and led him through the crowd, down the stairs into the kitchen of Cal's. Instantly, he started to cry. Through his distorted, ugly cry face and gaps for air, he began to tell me all about how he was being mistreated. I stopped him and told him that crying here, tonight, was social suicide. Fuck not getting into the frat, the students outside of the frat would also hear about it. He liked to be seen, so he would be seen crying. Fuck not getting laid tonight, he better get used to not getting laid for the next four years. He panted some and calmed down. I knew where the bottle of whiskey for the kitchen guys was stashed and I went over and grabbed it. I took a swig and passed it to Les. I went to pat him on the back and he awkwardly hugged me. He made it through that night and got into Kappa later that semester.

I look around the Whole in the Wall. Two of the TVs turn on then back off. The cash register also turns off immediately after I put in my password to open up the menu screen. How did I get here? How did I get back here? I hate this bar. I hate the mundane small talk with the old men in the afternoon. I hate the dumb questions from tourists. I hate how, at some point this evening, some stranger will tell me I don't look happy. That night when I met Les at Cal's, I was still happy bartending.

It wasn't long before Les lost the little humility he came into his freshman year with. Over the next couple of years, I saw him at least four or five times a week at Cal's. Some days it was on one of my afternoon shifts where he would come in and nurse a couple of beers while taking breaks from his advanced calculus equations to brag to me about all the pussy he was getting on the nights he didn't come into Cal's. Other days it was on weekend nights when he would come in wearing a button-up with one too many buttons open, put down his card, and make it very clear which people could order on his card and which people couldn't. Either way, the tips were always enormous, which made him tolerable. My habits weren't cheap. He was arrogant and loud. He was shallow and crass. The rest of the staff at Cal's who weren't getting his tips loathed him. You could tell it was the same with his peers. They tolerated him because he would overcompensate with his father's black card. There were times I would watch the Kappa brothers and their female counterparts mock him right to his face while he picked up the entire tab and I would wonder who was worse, him or them.

There were a few times, on rainy afternoons while the bar was slow, that Les would talk to me about his childhood or his schoolwork. Of course, when it came to his schoolwork, I never had even a slight understanding of what he was talking about. I couldn't even pass algebra in high school. He had been regarded as some sort of math prodigy growing up. When he talked to me about his work, he would blink furiously and pace in circles around his barstool. He told me his achievements and scholarships as a young man had been the only time he had received any type of attention from his family. The way he described his childhood made me sad. He was raised mostly by nannies, a father who would only acknowledge him when he would accomplish something, and a mother who apparently didn't care at all. They never called him, never came to visit, and according to him, were relieved to have him out of the house. Les was certainly annoying, but it's your family, if nobody else, who is supposed to learn to love those annoyances. It seemed from childhood and now into his college years, no one had ever just liked Les for Les—I certainly didn't.

But over the years, as the upperclassmen left and new scrawny white boys in argyle and boat shoes came into the frat, any hope for empathy and kindness I had hoped for out of Les, based on his early experience, dissipated. He was cruel to the pledges, doing things like spitting in their drinks when they weren't looking and making off-color jokes about them to their faces while the other brothers cringed and forced smiles, hoping Les would pick up their tab. There were a few senior brothers who came from similar financial standings as Les and they didn't care about his money. They were brutal to him. Any time he would poke fun at a pledge, they would pounce on him verbally and knock him back down. They still managed to make it onto his bar tab. Somehow, unbeknownst to him, he had become the frat clown with the endless wallet, and from the rumors I was hearing, he wasn't just picking up bar tabs anymore. He was buying hotel rooms at the plaza and prostitutes for the senior brothers while supplying the entire frat with coke. Now when he would come in on weekend nights to "Club Cal's," his outfits were gaudy by Kanye West's standards and he was louder and more obnoxious than ever. Even though I knew him beyond all this, I couldn't stomach it and would make the newer bartenders deal with him.

One afternoon he came in frantic—he'd been cut off. Apparently, on alumni night he brought a dozen or so guys to a strip club and dropped over twenty grand. When his father saw the charge, he froze all his accounts. Les ranted over this injustice as I poured us a couple shots. He looked through me while he spoke, not once making eye contact. He drank three beers while occasionally getting up and throwing his hands against the wooden bar, then walking out front for a smoke. After a couple of hours, he grew silent, then asked to pay. I charged him for two beers and took care of the rest. He paid with a twenty and fondled the four dollars in change for a moment before handing me two.

Over the next few weeks, all I heard of Les was hearsay. He had gotten a part-time job at a copy and print store for petty cash. His father still paid his room and board and his tuition, but his accounts stayed frozen. Rumor had it he wasn't taking the change well. There was a story going around that he had lashed out at his fraternity president over some minor policy dispute. He had also lashed out physically at the girl he was dating at a party. Some Kappa brothers sat at the bar late one night. I let a few of them stay after hours while I cleaned, and I eavesdropped as they discussed what to do about Les. I heard one brother literally say he was useless to them without his funds. Before the end of the semester, word was he was kicked out of the frat. It all happened so fast, in a matter of a few weeks. He may have been in a complete downward spiral, but regardless, it was clear. Les with no money defeated the purpose of Les. He didn't come into Cal's once during this time.

On the night of Kappa's annual graduation buyout, I expected Les to show up, although none of the brothers in the frat agreed with me. I knew he wouldn't be able to just let it go. And I was right. At about 1:00 a.m., while the party was at the height of its absurdity, I went out for a cigarette and saw Les meandering down the street alone.

"Ha! You would be working this," he croaked at me.

"Les...it's been awhile, man. What's up?" I said in a concerned tone.

"Oh, like you haven't heard all about it. They've told you. Those fuckin' liars told you."

"You aren't trying to go in there, are you Les?"

"What? I can't see my brothers?" he said sarcastically, his words slurring.

"Come on, man. You don't want to go see everybody like this." Les stood, swaying, trying to keep me in focus. Then, for the second time since I met him, he started crying. I took him by the elbow and walked him around the corner, off Broadway. "Dude. You still have next year, man. You're a smart kid, maybe the smartest I know. You're going to bounce back from this. Just go get some sleep." He tried speaking but his words were muffled by his pathetic whimpering. "Hey man. The last thing you want is for one of these guys to round this corner and see you crying. You have to pull yourself together." Les nodded, and without saying anything else, turned away from me and walked down the dark side street away from Broadway. It would be almost three years before I would see Les again.

I left Cal's before the summer was over for my second stint in rehab. Everything I heard of Les' senior year I heard from my friend Steve who still worked at Cal's. Apparently, he came back senior year already securing a job for after graduation with a major tech company,

73

with a beautiful Russian sweetheart he met abroad, his own apartment off campus, and a vendetta against Kappa. Steve told me how he would go around outbidding Kappa for open bars and just show up with his girlfriend and one or two other people and hang out in the empty space. I don't know how he had so much money again. I didn't know if his father had given him reign again on some accounts, or if Les had made some money on his own. Honestly, I didn't care much. I was now in and out of rehab, living in halfway houses, and working in a warehouse. My old customers were fleeting thoughts and I would change the channel on them almost immediately if I tuned in.

After multiple slips and some failed attempts, I had just over two years sober when I saw Les again. I was working for my Aunt Riley at the Major Network. I'd completed the three-month inpatient rehab (my third), followed by the six-month outpatient rehab, and had stayed sober another year on top of that. All of this was a pre-requisite for her giving me a job. She finally gave me a shot to use that long-lost communications degree I'd received ten years earlier. I wouldn't go so far as to say I was happy, but I was okay for the first time in a long time. I had a little place, a small savings, and I'd even come to terms with Lila leaving me almost two years earlier.

One day I walked out of work for my lunch and there he was. It took me a few moments to recognize him. He was wearing a suit with no tie and the top three shirt buttons undone. He had filled in around the shoulders and chest. He stood half-leaning on an Italian sports car. Upon seeing me, he took off his designer sunglasses and smiled at me like he had just revealed the punchline of a dirty joke.

"Les. Wow, look at you." I approached, surprised, and reached out my hand. He said nothing and went in for a hug.

"What are you doing for lunch, my man? I want to take you out."

"How did you know I was here? I—"

"Who cares!" he interrupted. "Here we are. Come on. Jump in." I went to make an excuse, but I had no lunch plans and I guess I was curious to see him. I suppressed my confusion of him finding me at the Major Network and got in the car.

He drove erratically, all brakes and gas. I felt like I would be sick. I had so many questions to ask him, but something about him made me feel inverted and nervous. He spoke almost non-stop about himself, about women and money, surface-level bragging—nothing at all surprising from Les. We pulled into a parking garage on the Upper East Side. He got out and handed his keys to an attendant whom he said nothing to and who simply nodded at Les in return. He walked a pace in front of me looking back over his shoulder talking about how good it was to see me. Do I remember this and that? Have I heard from him or her? Even if I wanted to, which I didn't, I couldn't get a word in.

The hostess knew him and brought him to a banquette that overlooked Park Avenue. The server came over no less than ten seconds after we sat down to take a drink order.

"Good afternoon sweetheart," he said, looking her up and down. "I will have two," he paused to show his sincerity. "Grey Goose martinis, dry, and an espresso." He looked over at me. "And what are you drinking these days? A Shirley Temple?" He laughed and grabbed me on the arm playfully. I wondered how he knew I was sober.

"I'll take a club soda. Thanks."

Les continued to make small, fast, one-sided talk while we waited for the drinks. The server put a martini in front of each of us and Les corrected her only by pointing at the cocktail in front of me and then pointing to the space in front of him. After she moved the second martini in front of him, he looked at her violently and shooed her away with his hand. He leaned into one of the martinis and started loudly slurping until it was a quarter of the way gone, picked it up, and finished it. He smiled painfully at me and took a sip of espresso. I braced myself for more words, but he just sat there, completely still, looking at me. I felt an awkward urge to speak.

"So, Les. It seems like you are doing pretty well these days. What are you—"

"I want your help." He was suddenly all business. "I know it's been a while, but I don't trust many people and right now, I need someone I can trust."

"What's up? I don't know if there is much I can do for a guy like you, Les, but hopefully I can help." I remembered how much I didn't miss being around him. His insecurity and his arrogance had grown worse by some sort of success. Whatever his achievements were, they didn't take away the anger and fear from his personality and it still showed in his eyes.

"I'm sure you can tell by now that I've sought you out." He leaned back towards the table, attacking his second martini, but this time he stopped after draining the top inch of liquid. "I know you have been through a lot. You know, with the drugs and the rehabs and everything. It's all fine. I'm not judging you. I will never forget what you did for me back when I was in school. I looked into you. I think I can help you. And I know you can help me."

"Dude," I impatiently interjected. "A few things, man. How did you 'look into me?' And I don't think there is much I can do for you, Les." He sat and looked at me seriously.

"Please don't interrupt me." At this, I almost stood up and walked out. I wasn't going to be spoken to like this, not by Les. I think he noticed I was becoming annoyed and his face went from intense to playful in an instant. "Listen, I just need you to test out an app I designed." He shrugged his shoulders and held his hands out to the side over his shoulders, palms up. "No big deal, right? I don't know why you seem so defensive." He grabbed my arm again in that spirited way he had when asking what I was drinking.

If I was defensive, I can't explain exactly why I was. Les made me uncomfortable, but not ever in a threatening way. He was altogether harmless. He was overbearing and insecure, unpredictable and annoying, but I never felt directly threatened by him. What I was afraid of, was opening a gateway to having to see him regularly. I knew he couldn't have had many friends. How could he? He was awful. I saw the way he had looked at me in college. I knew he looked up to me. I knew he believed I cared about him. I couldn't accept the fact he that had "sought me out," spied on me. It just goes to show how off-center Les was.

"I don't think I'm the right guy, dude." My tone was now superior sounding, like the cool older kid I wanted to be seen as by Les. I felt in control. Fuck the money and the car, he was still just Les.

"I will give you seventy-five thousand dollars. Cash." He said coldly, picking up on my tone of superiority and swatting it off.

"How do you... Why?" I felt my body language stutter.

"My father died a few years back, so the money is whatever, really. I have a ton of it. So I've designed an app, and it's going to be big. You have no idea how big it can be. I just need someone I trust to test it, and I don't trust many people. I don't really trust anyone if I can be honest.

"And you trust me?"

"Of course! You were always real with me. You were always nice to me." He emphasized the word nice, then finished his second martini.

I thought about it briefly, sitting across from him. Why not? It's true, I didn't like Les, but I had no reason to screw him over. And seventy-five thousand dollars in cash was a hell of a lot of money.

"You can trust me. Yeah, of course."

Les smiled and put his hand on top of mine and double-clicked it like a computer mouse. He spotted the server walking to the neighboring table.

"One more martini," he said loudly without looking her way. She looked back at him and smiled while her eyes filled with contempt. There was an uncomfortable silence between us.

"So, what is it, Les? Tell me about the app."

"It's called Distance. It's like a game in a sense, using GPS and in a way, virtual reality. The kinks need to be worked out but it's almost ready. The objective of the app itself is a good deal away from realized, but the important part, the technology, the parts I can't explain to you because you wouldn't understand, no offense, but also because it's possibly the most fragile, valuable interface in the world, is fuckin' ready to go, my man. It's top notch—there is nothing else like it that exists, my man. No one knows it but me and I intend to keep it that way. It's the crux of whatever stupid game we'll build around it. It's the key to all of it."

"I don't think I follow you, Les."

"And you don't have to. All you have to do is let me download it to your phone. I'll drop you back at work, but I need your phone for a couple hours. I'll pick you back up at six and it'll be on your cell. I'll give you twenty-five K up front, like now, and when I bring back the phone all you have to do is sign in. It will read your fingerprint and you'll be in. All you need to do is log in and follow the instructions until the end and then I will meet you with the other fifty K."

Les pulled an ink pad and a pink sheet of paper out of his pocket and put them on the table. The server came and dropped off his martini. He didn't say thank you.

"This all sounds a little intrusive." To this, Les let out a howl of a laugh. People from the other tables look over at us.

"Please. If I needed to spy on you or be 'intrusive,' or whatever, I wouldn't need to do this. Here, take this now." He pulled out an envelope and pushed it gently into my ribs.

He dropped me back off at work and for the remaining three hours of the day, I couldn't concentrate. I went into a bathroom stall and counted the cash. Twenty-five thousand dollars—all hundred-dollar bills. For the rest of the day, I kept my hand in my pocket, gripping the envelope. The time crawled by. I thought about what I could do with the money and what I couldn't do. Something felt illegal about it. I was flushed red and anxious. All I knew was I wanted to get it home and get it safe.

At 5:58, I started out of the office and into the street where I had met Les earlier. He was waiting for me, holding the same casual pose he had earlier that afternoon.

"My man!" His eyes were wide and energetic but also a little lazy. He looked simultaneously wired and sleepy. He handed me the phone. "Easy enough, no?" It all felt unreal, like a dream. I had this gnawing sense I was doing something criminal but couldn't think of what that was.

"Yeah, easy. So I just open it up tonight and what, play the game? And then call you or—"

"Relax, relax. First things first, my man. I need you to sign this. You can read it over or whatever. It just says that if you don't finish, or if you tell anyone about the app, you don't get the fifty K. The money in your pocket is yours. Don't spend that shit in one place, my man!"

I grabbed the paper. One sheet. I started to skim it and although I was reading it, my mind was moving so fast, in so many directions at once, I couldn't retain it all. But from what I gathered, it was exactly what Les said it was—finish the instructions and keep it to myself, or I forfeit the second payment.

"Don't worry. I trust you." He looked at me earnestly for maybe the first time since I'd known him.

I signed the document. He extended his hand to me and I shook it. His hands were clammy and cold. He walked around to the driver side of his car.

"Are you okay to drive, Les?"

He looked back at me with a wicked-looking grin. "Oh, fuck off, Dad."

The tumblers atop the ice machine rattle as it hums back into autorun to make more ice. The ice machine is something he can't control, at least I don't think. Control: an unhinged concept wrapped around the opposite of what it really is. There is no order to be maintained. I look at my phone resting on the bar and it's turning on and off on repeat. The same thing is happening to the bar's cash register. I don't bother checking the computer in the office downstairs. He's probably bored and drunk. Drunk and without a friend to take hostage of.

I pour myself a shot of whiskey then empty the bitter contents of the sweaty cider bottle down my throat. It's warmish and slimy at the end. Les' visit today makes me think of Distance and ruins the relief of the booze. Booze: the last-straw substance—the "it'll have to do" remedy. Ask any feign, dopehead, or junkie about the effects of alcohol when they're craving their drug of choice. It becomes a hot, heavy, laborious battle just to make do, a bowel-antagonizing slug that reminds you that you can't have what you really want, but that you can't be left sober either. The exception being whiskey. Thank god for whiskey.

That first night, I opened Distance back at my apartment without a clue, focused only on the cash stuffed deep in my closet and the cash to be had. Even as I opened the app and let it read my fingerprint, I thought about how at one point in the not too distant past, a phone was just a phone. At that moment, the app was just an app.

While I was on the subway home that night, it must have rained, and rained hard. The rest of the evening was steamy and when the sun went down it turned to fog. I pulled a half-eaten pint of Haagen-Dazs out of my freezer, turned on the TV, and picked up my phone. I looked at the icon, a little red square with a lowercase d, and started thinking about how insane this all was. Les, the money, the ambiguity of the app itself—some kind of GPS "game?"

I clicked on the icon and a shade of red eclipsed the screen. In a simple Courier-type font, the name of the app, *distance*, shone in white. Below was a generic fingerprint also outlined in white, and below that, it read: Your Fingerprint Please. My home button glowed white, something I hadn't seen it do before, and I started thinking maybe the technology Les was using really was advanced. I put my thumb on the home button and a series of flashes and text appeared on the screen. I was instantly overwhelmed and reached for my TV's remote in a hurry to turn it off. A wave of excitement flooded over me. I felt moved enough to give my best efforts to testing out this app. After all, Les had trusted me and was giving me a generous amount of cash. I might as well give it a first-rate effort. Who knows what future opportunities could come from this? I was sitting on the edge of my couch now, attentive.

The instructions welcomed me by name to: *Distance, A Game of Finding.* I hadn't been asked to input my name but figured Les had done it when he'd had my phone. It asked me to apply my fingerprint again, and this time for longer and with my index finger. I felt delighted for Les, proud of him. Nothing had even happened yet, and I was oddly gripped. Distance seemed to be calculating something and I was entranced by the buffering symbol of a duck slowly appearing then disappearing on my screen. I felt safe and warm, like I was in the right place, doing the right thing. *Would You Like To Take A Walk?* The words brushed up lightly against the inside of my phone like they had been carried by a breeze from some deep place to find a comfortable resting area on my screen.

As I was putting on my shoes, I looked over at my now melted ice cream. I thought about how if you don't take advantage of something beautiful, something as beautiful and caring as ice cream, it will change and become something useless. But that was okay. That's life. The missed opportunities in life are really just lessons, aren't they? Looking at the melted ice cream, I wanted to cry, cry over the delicacy of it, it's waste.

The way the mist felt on my face when I walked out of my apartment flooded me with the short, rapid breaths you get when you jump into cold water. The fog created the feeling of an odyssey like the city was some medieval landscape I was to trudge through to slay a dragon and save a princess, or get lost in and find some beautiful crystal. It was a bustling Thursday night and the energy of my neighborhood was unmatchable. People together, people separately together and unique, all apart moving from place to place with what they believed were destinations, but in reality were just dances. The human mistake that we had any actual objectives was suddenly clear and the beauty in finally seeing that was unparalleled.

Let's Take A Left. We Are Going To Find Where You Need To Be. I felt the city breathe. I felt the pulse from people's past as I walked through the mist that was the breath of their future. The cars stood still while the street moved. I walked down streets I had avoided for no reason since I moved to this neighborhood. I studied the outsides of different restaurants and grocery stores finding the similarities and uniquenesses in them that made them both of New York and loyal to their owner's homelands. I don't know how long I was meandering. It felt like minutes and hours equally. Before I knew it, the locations started to become familiar again while remaining confusingly distant and unworldly. Abruptly, I was on my street again, approaching my apartment from the opposite way I had walked out of it. Distance had taken me in a circle and I hadn't noticed. *We Are So Close To Finding Where You Need To Be* illuminated my screen, but more hollow and blurry than the other instructions had been. It quickly grew dimmer and then exited itself.

I was standing in front of my building staring at my home screen. I clicked on the app. It didn't open. As I walked up the steps my apartment, my legs felt heavy, as if they were weighed down with toddlers grabbing at my jeans. When I sat back down on my couch, the air felt stuffy, dry, and uncomfortably warm. I clicked on the app again and it didn't open. I rapidly kept clicking and even thought about calling Les to let him know it wasn't opening. I wiped the sweat from my forehead and took a breath. *No. This was the point. When I see him next, I will explain to him that it worked very well for a while then stopped working altogether.* But what worked well for a while?

I stood over the toilet with an uncomfortable urge to pee. Nothing more than a few drops came out, but the urge didn't go away. I was thirsty but felt almost guilty drinking water with this sensation in my bladder. As I chugged water in my kitchen, I looked over at the melted remnants of my ice cream. It made me want to vomit. It looked like sludge or oil and I couldn't believe I had attempted to eat any form of what that was. I dumped it in the kitchen sink and watched it grease the metal like a moving slime. I rinsed it away, relieved to see it gone but only relieved for a minute or so before I was standing over the toilet trying to pee again. After getting nowhere in the bathroom, I wet a rag and laid on my bed with the fan pointing at me. I went in and out of consciousness for a few hours, never really falling asleep.

The next day at work I felt sluggish. Going against my reasoning from the night before, I called Les on my lunch break. No answer. I called him before heading back into work and again, nothing. I couldn't concentrate at all on what I was supposed to be working on at the Major Network. I took two breaks that afternoon to call Les, but he didn't answer either of them. On my way home from work, I called him for a fifth time with the same results. I felt like an overzealous date or a guy waiting on his dealer. Dozens of times that day I looked at the icon. It was a faded pinkish-red now, and the d looked distant and blurry. When I clicked on it, it would bounce but not open.

Around 6:30, when I was getting off the train in my neighborhood, I saw I had one new text message from Les. *Can't talk. We will meet up next week to go over d.*

I sent him a wordy text about how it wasn't opening. He didn't respond. By the time I arrived home after stopping to get cigarettes and a microwaveable pizza (which didn't seem appetizing, but I hadn't been able to eat all day) I received another text from Les.

Don't worry.

I showered, sat on my couch, and put on some mindless sitcom. I couldn't sit still. I toyed with the idea of going to an NA meeting but thought I would only be more jittery in that room and my fellows in sobriety might think I was on drugs again, prompting relentless calling and texting for the foreseeable future. I thought about calling the girl I had recently been out with, the girl from the dating app, but that idea went away as quickly as it came. I forged a brief idea that I could call Lila. I never actually believed it. If I did call her, maybe I could show her this "billion-dollar idea" that yours truly was now in on.

Around 8:00, I started cleaning my kitchen. I would start wiping down one area and stop mid-wipe to move some dishes around or take out the garbage. No one chore was being accomplished.

Then I heard an unfamiliar ping from across the room. My phone was on the coffee table in the living room and when I walked over and picked it up, there was a bright red banner glowing in flashes across the top. *One New Message From Distance. Are You Ready To Go A Further Distance?* My heart raced. Looking back, something happened next that should have drawn my attention, should have made me detect everything that was wrong with Distance. My thumb spasmed. I applied my twitching thumb to the home button and held it there until the app opened.

I don't remember leaving my apartment or the exact places I went that night or the next. I know I slept most of the day Saturday. I know that when I wasn't logged in, when I wasn't able to log in, I couldn't quite describe the point of Distance to myself, but when I was in I didn't have to explain it. As cliché as it sounds, it wasn't about the destination, it was about the journey. I was out in my city, feeling at one with who I was and who the city was, what we should be. Each play, each trip, was a little shorter and left me more exhausted than the last. It seemed like a matter of hours before my alarm was stabbing the inside of my eardrums Monday morning. When I would get a chance to talk to Les, I knew what my feedback would be. He needed to improve the strength of the signal. Thursday night's play was the most intense and each night it had become less extraordinary. Potency was the word that kept coming to mind, although I knew it wasn't right.

I suffered through my Monday shift. By 2:00 p.m., I had to tell my boss I wasn't feeling well and had to go home. "You don't look well. Get some rest." On my way home I received a text from Les. *I will see you Thursday afternoon.* I had such a small amount of energy at that moment all I could type back was, *OK.*

Monday night, the ping was almost inaudible. If I hadn't been on high alert for it, I would have missed it. The play lasted all of twenty minutes and I was consciously aware that the game would end the whole time. Its suggestions on where to go were vague and the gusto behind the game was all wrong. Whatever groundbreaking software Les had programmed into Distance was wearing off and wearing off fast. Even though it had only been a part of my life for a few days, I felt slighted. I was angry. In the hours after the play ended Monday night, I felt this confusing hatred for Les, while I yearned for him to make it okay. I went to call him, to ask him where he was so I could come tell him it wasn't working so he could fix it. I felt too weak to make that call. I put my fan on full blast, put a wet towel on my head, and got into bed. I was too agitated to sleep but too tired to get up.

Tuesday, I called out of work and stayed in bed. I pined to hear the ping on my phone, a ping that never came. The icon was ghostly-looking now. I had to squint to see the pinkish- white square. I couldn't get comfortable. I also didn't want to get up. I took agonizing steps into my bathroom and sat on the floor of my shower. I let the water pour over my face and at one point felt as if I was drowning. I noticed mold on the ceiling that I hadn't seen before, smells I hadn't noticed. I felt a mix of anger and lethargy that left me feeling simply pathetic.

Wednesday morning, after calling out of work again, I received a call from my aunt. She had heard about me being sick and not being able to come to work at the Major Network at all that week. She asked me if I needed anything, wished me well, but then added, "I hate to say this to you sweetheart, but I feel it's my responsibility. If this is at all drug-related, there are going to be major, major problems. One of them being, you will be out of a job." I assured her it wasn't and went back to bed.

As I drifted off in bed that afternoon, I started to become aware of the absurdity of all this. Was I feeling sick because of the app? Or more accurately, the lack thereof? I couldn't be. I must have coincidently come down with something. But if so, then what? I wouldn't allow myself to become too caught up in what seemed to be impossible narratives. I didn't have the energy. While I was asleep, I suffered from a brutal bout of sleep paralysis. I could feel myself awake in my bed, head facing up, arms at my side. I saw the dimensions of the room and a couple of times even felt as if I was up walking around, carrying a deep-seeded knowledge that I was still lying there. I tried to scream out. I tried moving my arm to punch the wall. Nothing was working. Eventually, after what felt like hours, I was truly awakened by an ear-piercing ping and a blanket of blinding red light. It took me a few seconds, now sitting forward gasping for air, covered in sweat, to escape the ringing and crimson. After a series of violent breaths, I put my feet on the floor. I felt cold in the places I had sweat and flushed in all the others. I gravitated to my phone. It was so bright I couldn't look at it directly. It flashed, *Upgrade Due. Press And Hold.* There wasn't even a moment of hesitation before my thumb was against the home button.

In a matter of seconds, any doubt of where my affliction was coming from was squashed like a bug in front of a girlfriend. My bedroom, the place I slept every night for years, was suddenly different, unfamiliar in the best way. It was alive, like a dinner party full of intellectuals while there remained a keen awareness that it was just me. My solitude felt rich with companionship. Distance was less telling me where to go as it was guiding me. I hit the technicolor outside with an eagerness that I had never felt before. The journey, the voyage, the distance that was Distance soaring along with me.

Unlike the past version of Distance, this updated edition took me far out of my surroundings. Where the first edition had me in tune with my surroundings, this new one had a welcomed disconnect. I felt I was acting out scenarios that couldn't be true. My neighborhood felt like a stage and the residents felt like actors. People were not passing me as much as entering then exiting me. The sky was full of almost neon colors and the clouds had sharp shapes as they sped past me. I felt an unnatural speed to my movements and my heart was racing, albeit calmly. I felt wrong and I fuckin' loved it. But as I continued to play, the effect was becoming too much. I was losing track of time and although I was elated and intoxicated, I was starting to feel a panic. With matching intensity, I would snap out of it, only for a second, and see the dull colors of the real world and the horror that I was far from my apartment and unable to manage my own movement. Each time, without hitting anything on my phone, I would snap back into Distance and it would be more intense. I had this internal dialogue that was pleading for it to stop—words to myself of relapse. I hadn't relapsed. I hadn't had anything to drink. I hadn't done any drugs. I was just playing a game. I was testing an app for a friend. But there was a growing reality that I was as high as I had ever been in my life. I was fucked up.

My surroundings started to become familiar in my jolts back to reality. I was in a different borough, but I had lived here once—this was home once. I was inside now and I wasn't alone. During a long two- to three-second burst to reality, I saw where I was and I was horrified. As I fell back into Distance, I reached into my pocket and grabbed my phone and with every bit of strength I had in me, I threw it. There was a sound of breaking glass as my phone went through a window and the room dimmed and hummed like a giant computer that was violently unplugged. In front of me was Lila's best friend, Amy. She was shouting, and as I came to, she went from muted to agonizingly loud. "Get the fuck out of here, you fucking maniac!" she screamed as her closed fists bounced off my chest and arms. All the feeling rushed back into me. "The cops are coming, you psycho!"

I looked around. I was in my old apartment. There was a dinner party happening. All ten or so guests paused, motionless, silent. Some guy with a big nose and slicked black hair had my bicep grasped in his hand, his face too close to mine, and was trying to pull me out. I started to turn my head and caught my reflection in the full-size mirror in the corner. There I was, shirtless, the top half of my body leaning forward, dangling above the bottom half with blood all over my lips and chin. I could only look for a moment before I had to look away and that's when I saw Lila in the corner being guarded by some friends. She was crying and looking at me with a ghastly look I had never seen in our seven years together. She was on the phone. She was repeating her address.

I ran out the front door and down the stairs. It was dark out now. I saw my ripped shirt on the sidewalk outside of Lila's place. I picked it up and couldn't put it back on, it was too mangled to wear. I got about two blocks away before I became suddenly sick. I vomited behind a dumpster. I felt like I might shit my pants. A wave of heat disabled me. I saw Prospect Park in the distance, a few blocks away, and I hobbled there like a zombie, shooting pains stabbing my left shin. I had no way to know the time, but by the lack of people about I could tell it was late, probably after midnight, hours since I signed back into Distance. I disgustingly and urgently evacuated my bowels in the park and not too far from that exact spot, laid down on my side and fell asleep behind a bush.

I was up and stumbling to my feet before I was even fully awake. The side I had passed out on was covered with dew and grass and dirt. Dull flashes of the night before were drifting through my brain while I concentrated on not vomiting. I stood filthy and shirtless on the sidewalk and tried to hail a cab back to my apartment, but none would pick me up. I didn't have any cash on me anyway if they did. After a few minutes, I asked a terrified pedestrian the way to the subway and then stood outside the turnstile, humiliated, asking if anyone could swipe me in.

The subway was cold. Air conditioning pumped out onto my bare shoulders. I tucked my chest into my knees to fight the nausea. It felt like hours before I arrived at my stop. I had to knock on my super's door to get her to let me into my apartment. It surprised me how quickly I became accustomed to feeling humiliated. The first thing I did once inside was vomit and shit until I had nothing left to give. Then I went and checked on the money. All there. I saw my alarm clock out of the corner of my eye. I should have been at work three hours ago and of course, I hadn't called. What I needed to do was get dressed and go straight to my aunt's office. There was no point in trying to talk to my immediate superior. I showered, dressed, and took nine hundred-dollar bills and stuck them into my pocket. Feeling the cash in my hand reminded me it was Thursday. I'd see Les today.

I moved past each cubicle like a mist that silenced any and all

85

conversation. I felt a quiver in my steps, a weakness in my knees as I approached my aunt's corner office. She was on the phone, so I stuck just the top half of my body in the doorway. She looked up at me, then quickly back down at her desk while she yessed whoever was on the other line. She hung up and still didn't look at me. I went to speak and was cut off.

"Please," she said, holding up her index finger, finally looking at me. "The police were here today. You are very lucky Lila has decided not to press charges. Nevertheless, they wanted to speak to you, but since you weren't here they asked me if I would, so here we are." I went to speak again and she cut me off, raising that same finger. "And I will speak to you. I will speak to you as your aunt, but I will only do that after you finish treatment. As your employer, I am asking you to leave. You no longer work here. Do not," she said with added volume, "say a word to me or anyone else. Do not go to your desk. This morning, this week, has been embarrassing enough. I do not want to have to call security, but I will if you say one fucking word to me right now." With that, she looked at me with the eyes of a boxer before a match. As much as I wanted to explain, to plead with her, I had my hand on the bills in my pocket and decided that I would be able to get by for a while until things cooled down. Then I would be able to explain myself to her. I turned and left the Major Network.

On the way down the elevator, it felt like a thousand thoughts were trying to enter my brain at once, each being jammed up by the other. I would go home and wait for Les. I was sure he'd know I was not at work. I still had most of the twenty-five thousand and I'd get the rest from Les when we met. Then I'd leave town. My thoughts were impulsive and erratic, but so was I.

When I walked out of the Major Network, he was leaning against his car the same way he had a week earlier. The sight of him made me want to run at him and knock his head off his shoulders. He wore that smug look like nothing was wrong, but when I looked in his beady little eyes, I saw it. I saw that he knew. He'd known all along.

"Woof! You look like shit, my man."

I was too weak and too angry to speak. As I walked past Les, I looked him in his greyish-green eyes and for a moment he was that crying college freshman. I sat in the car and slammed the door behind me.

My senses felt less acute than ever, but also more fragile—the restaurant was too bright, the sounds of plates and silverware clanking together was deafening while people's voices, including Les', seemed faded. On top of that, my mouth was dry and I felt nauseous.

The entire drive there, Les remained uncharacteristically quiet. I kept my attention out the window and did my best not to show how sick I was feeling. Now, sitting in the banquette, Les looked at me directly for the first time. I felt the redness and width of my eyes in that moment.

"The update was a bit much, I realize that now. We're working the bugs out as we speak. When you reopen it, you'll see. We've worked it out." He looked around for the waitress.

"Reopen it?" The sound of my own vibrating voice caught me off guard. I was leaning towards him, both fists clenched. "You knew. You fucking rat." I felt the spit coming off my tongue as I hissed at him. I hadn't expected to get here this fast. I wanted an explanation from him first, but the second I saw his face outside the Major Network I knew why he'd asked me. "You knew this would happen to me. You asked me, me specifically, because you knew."

"Hey. C'mon now, my man..." Les was shaking his head from side to side slowly, squinting his eyes at me with a sour look of misunderstanding, but then he stopped abruptly. His shoulders relaxed and his face went stoic. He rolled his eyes quickly. "Fuck it. Can't do it. Fine. You're right. I did know you'd get like this. And do you know why that is? Because you are a fuckin' junkie. And do you know what this is?" He pointed to his phone. "This is a drug. No. No. It's better than a drug. It's the future of drugs. And just like if dating apps couldn't hook lonely fucks, and if delivery apps couldn't hook lazy fat fucks, what good is a drug app that can't hook an addict fuck like you?" He let out a long sigh and pulled at the edges of his collar. All the outrage left me. I felt weighed down.

"Why would you do this to me? After all—"

"After what?" Les interrupted, looking as if he ate something nasty. "After you served me drinks? And took my generous tips and paid your rent and fed your habits, then after I had no money, just let me disappear? You had less loyalty than the rest of them. You were worse than them. At least the rest of those people treated me like they couldn't stand me. You pretended to care about me." He then started laughing this forced, blustery laugh. It was cut short. I hadn't grasped what happened until I was easing back into my seat and wiping the blood off my knuckles. It happened so fast, mid-chuckle, that he didn't let out a noise until his head was falling back forward and a high-pitched groan emitted from him. He covered his nose and mouth. I had managed to strike him twice in quick succession without any other customers or restaurant staff noticing. I finished wiping my hands as he put his napkin to his face. Then he howled like a child. The staff was frozen in place as I got up and walked across the dining room. The hostess smiled at me as I walked out of the restaurant.

Mixing alcohol with a Distance withdrawal was like covering my entire body with an uncomfortable static—a low energy, constant electric shock. But after a few days, drinking was just drinking again. I left town. There were trains and cheap motel rooms and the easy access to drugs that exists when you are looking for them. I paid my cousin and his friend too much of my money to put my belongings into storage and clean out my apartment. It wasn't as hard as I imagined to blow through twenty-five thousand dollars. I found the Whole in the Wall job before I even returned to New York. The owner was a friend of an old drinking buddy. I found a room to rent not far away.

Les checked in the first day I bought a new iPhone. He never directly contacted me. He would do things instead like shut off my phone or change my passwords. I could feel the boredom and midday intoxication in his pranks. I liked to picture him drinking alone while he hacked me. What I still can't figure out is if he really did feel slighted by me and wanted some kind of revenge, or if he just wanted to justify his decision to use me.

A sheet of ice falls from the top of the machine making a pleasant little crash into the rest of the ice. At that exact moment, all the TVs in the Whole start flashing on and off, the music starts and stops rapidly—an orchestra of sight and noise. I move out from behind the bar and stand in the middle of the room amid the colors. All nine TVs are creating a tornado of fluorescent. The audio is heaving sharp jabs. I look at my phone, face up on the bar, it's also flashing red and white and there is a message. A chill runs through me. *Go Outside.* I walk out of the bar. It's right in front of me, the new advertisement on the bus stop across the street. I wonder if I missed it on my way into work.

A red poster with two smiling, captivated-looking young models. One's male, white, with blond hair, the other female, black, with shoulder-length curls. They are holding their phones in front of them and look to be exploring their surroundings. Above them reads: *Distance - An Interactive Virtual Reality Adventure For The Whole Family - Only Available On The New iPhone.*

FIRE ESCAPE

Sitting on my third fifth-story
fire escape,
I wonder why I can't remember my
old thoughts.
Were they real?
Have they changed?
Or are they all ( ) the same?

A third view of the same river.
Are my thoughts smaller
or have they grown bigger?
When they fade off my face,
they hang in the red reflected clouds.
Detected fluorescents off the Hudson's mirror.

It's a story more advanced,
with a smaller cast.
Is this what time brings?
Deeper thoughts
and fewer laughs.
To be more depraved but less
Obsessed.
I'm sorry, New York.
I'm just less impressed.

A LACK OF WORDS

A lack of words,
or in other terms,
a leap of faith,
into the rain,
out the way of
all that came before.
A sneaky bus
tailspins towards us
and right before,
like never before,
you see me blush.
What's left to say?
Let us try to explain.
If I asked you nicely,
would you teach me pain?

Would you believe
me if I told you
I'm not
afraid?
Now that I've learned
to sleep alone.
I don't need
to love myself.
Because do the rats?
Do the trees?

You,
so much more
interested in the universe.
Me, more concerned
with the soul.
We were both right
and both wrong.
We could never
hang on.
But in those moments
where the soul
and the universe met,
we gave each other things

we cannot give back.
It lit up rooms
that would eventually
burn me alive
without a chance
to say goodbye.

THE WIFE

I want to go back to a time
when the woman couldn't
leave the man.

No, you can't go,
because without me you can't stand,
let alone dance.

We can't talk about your dreams
if I don't let you sleep.
Keep persistent in your
trance and forget
about romance.

I am yours to
never leave.
And I will tell you when to
breathe.

BOOKMARK

A beautiful
woman once told me,
"Stop and look around."
But all I saw
was South Park and Pop-Tarts.
until there was this bookmark.

LONG BLONDE HAIR

Between the dope
fiends and Jesus freaks,
it seems to me
this liberty
is looking backwards
at my city's dream.
My own trilogy.
My brief history.

The eldest man in the family
died next.
Even so,
most of us were surprised.

Long blonde hair,
barely seventeen.
Craving to be seen.
Afraid
of how boys her age don't
please her.
I give in
and get beneath her.

I sit at a café
contemplating, considering, stalking.
Contemplating if
I should consider
stalking.
I hope when I wake up it's over.
I'm just feeling bored with feeling
bored,
of being sober.

SHADOW BOX

I sat in the common area by myself trying to read. This time around, I wasn't trying to make any friends. Instead of making conversations with the other patients, I sat there with the kind of half-smile a villain in an action movie wears the moment he realizes he is about to die. I had given up. I brought two books to read. Both were collections of short stories. One was by Roald Dahl and the other was by Raymond Carver. The only other people in the common area were a young woman around my age named Lydia and a man in his late fifties named Tyrone. They were both in my group.

Lydia was an attractive girl, about five-two with shoulder-length brown hair that she always kept tied into a short ponytail. She wore glasses and had a gaunt physique. She was a Jewish girl from Long Island and seemed harmless enough. Of the forty-some-odd people in the unit, she was one of the most disruptive. She was constantly going on about some ailment or another. Most recently, wax had been building up in her ear and she demanded to leave the unit to see a doctor. After multiple visits and no evidence of a build-up, she was back, but only until she decided it was time again to kick over some chairs and call the nurses bitches for not helping her in whatever crisis had come up. The only thing that seemed to calm her in these moments were threats of being moved to the psych ward.

Tyrone was a large black man. If I had to guess, I would say he was six-foot-four, 270 pounds. He had been in and out of prison since he was a teenager, mostly for selling drugs. He had been locked up in New York, Maryland, North Carolina, and Florida. Only in the past ten years or so had he begun to have problems with using drugs himself. I learned this information in the mandatory meetings that the three of us had to attend daily with the other patients. Tyrone was quiet. He did not talk much, only when he was called on by the counselor.

I sat reading while Lydia worked on a crossword puzzle, leaning over her knees that were pressed against her chest. She always seemed tense. Tyrone was looking out the window. It was raining. Then, as if bitten by something, Tyrone popped out of his chair. Both Lydia and I looked up from what we were doing. Before we could make sense of the change in the room, Tyrone started viciously shadow boxing the air. You could see the size and the power he carried. Quick jabs with breaths exaggerating each blow. His feet danced back and forth, and it was obvious he had done this before. He turned excitedly to each of us as if saying, "No more sitting still! It's time to move!" I gave my half-defeated smile while Lydia, who I assumed would protest the whole thing, began to laugh. Not the kind of playing along laughter I was forcing, but really laughing. Then Tyrone smiled. I realized I hadn't seen him smile. One of his front teeth had a gold rim around it. "Come on, little lady! Show me what you got!"

Lydia quickly got up. She started boxing back. Her legs didn't dance, they trotted up and down instead of back and forth. Tyrone laughed and showed her what she was doing wrong. She tried again, better this time. At least that's what Tyrone said, I didn't see much difference. The two of them now danced around each other. Lydia started to narrate the action.

The bout got intense. Lydia landed a jab to the chin. Tyrone jerked his head back then countered with a left to the body. The five-two Lydia landed a combo of fierce shots to the six-four Tyrone. Tyrone stumbled back, his head started to rotate on his shoulders. Then Lydia halted her awful footwork, wound up her now very loose body, and threw a haymaker. Tyrone let out a howl, spun around 360 degrees, and slowly fell to the tiles. As Tyrone acted out the most dramatic fall in boxing history, Lydia let out a laugh that could only come out of a child. She stood over him jumping with her hands raised above her head. She was making the sounds of a crowd gone wild. As she helped him up, he kept his hand on his knee. Then they hugged like two people who had missed each other for a long time.

The bell rang, followed by the sound of the other forty or so hungry patients coming down the hall.

FULL SUN

The fog makes it weirdly bright.
A full sun hanging
over the park.
I make out its border lines.
I walk into its sides.
I try to survive.

It's a central morning
on a central timeline.
Reactivate.
I sometimes still wonder
over your whereabouts.

Indirect steps towards
momentary encounters with
beautiful women
as if there were not buildings
on each side of this trail.

I wake up
in the center of the park.
My dog waits for me, smoking.
I tell him I can try.
I can pretend to remember your smell.
He says it's time to go home.
That all this is getting boring.
That nobody cares about me or
my story.

PAST

When the internet
existed
for conspiracy theories and
remixes,
I woke up
laying next to you
after an oxy-lovin' night,
waiting to start another fight.

I let you roll the blunt.
I let you sit up front.
You always sit next to me.
We took the back roads
through the green trees
past
the houses of our tired friends,
past
the girls who made you jealous,
past
the future lovers you'd take.
We'd drive past the future.

FOUNDATION

I miss the ocean but not the beach.
The sea of the truly wealthy and truly poor
float like flotsam in the city.
Somewhere between Brooklyn, New York, and Lynbrook, New York,
I search for
a sober piece of sand.
A sand castle made of stone rock.
An apartment embedded in sand.
Foundation unearthed from the slightest breeze.
The dope dealer's phone vibrates but he doesn't look,
his eyes deep-seeded in algae.
He's tired. He misses
her smell but not her voice.

SOMEWHERE BETWEEN CHARLES BUKOWSKI AND JESSE SCOTT OWEN

I put Blaine to bed on New Year's Eve.
She drank too much and tried to kiss me.
I wouldn't let her.
I took off her shoes and
wanted to take off her bra and slide my hand down the front of her
pants as she slept.
But I didn't do either.
My girlfriend was away on vacation in Europe.

I took the train to La Guardia just to see her in between flights.
We sat in the terminal.
She hadn't shaved her legs since she arrived in Asia six weeks earlier.
Maybe I would meet her in Boston.
But I'd have to take the bus.

ARGUE

When you were here,
you told me the past,
present, and future
always *were*.
I've learned
the past and future don't exist.
I see now you didn't
find all the answers
in your classroom and
from your friends.
Maybe expensive education
isn't worth the
pretension you carried with it.
And bitch,
maybe Einstein
was wrong.

KEEP MOVING

Keep moving
and where you're going
take me with you

This was a crazy turn
We've twisted a ripple
There were parts of my skin
alone in the sun
dried out
far past the point of a glisten

You walking in
was like a single drop
of water on a dried-out ground
Like a thunderstorm
that didn't make a sound

I've seen the other shoes drop
Twenty at once
Only to open my eyes
to a barrel of a gun

We are left as humans
with no choice but to keep
walking
towards a place we are not certain
exists

MARCH

March
gives birth then
kills off
the plants while
she figures out where she stands.
It's like that eerie journey of
not taking your own life
in your hands
and seeing where you land.
My friend Steve says,
"I was getting upset because I don't know who I am."
We talk about if we are complete
and the falsehoods of our interpretations of ourselves to ourselves.
Sometimes I have moments where nothing feels real.
I felt good
when Steve said,
"You are more than a book deal."

ARGENTINIAN TEENAGERS

Argentinian teenagers,
taking in the cities,
their predilections all
based in fiction.

Shocking green masses.

Turnstile seminars.

Debauchery hidden behind stars.

Captured innocence.

And they wonder,
Could this be New York?
The snow came and the snow
melts.
The only boy in the group
turns to his prettiest friend
and says,
"I'd rather end up in hell."

THE MINDS TRAVEL

I am so
tired of being cold
The wind blows
just inches off the ground
while I twist and turn
over conversations that
are over

The minds travel
It's what they see
It's in what they read
What now lives between
the covers of production manuals
and the roads inside lucid novels
They travel
for the sake of taking the same
route back
Home with more in their minds
so much more on their shoulders
and less time

I am so
tired of being mad

SUGAR

My head ached.
I drank some water and
cracked my joints.
It pulsed and it ached.

I got hard enough
to pull fast,
to the point,
and my head ached.

I let it out on her body.
I let my hands and my mouth
water and release—my heart beat.
It rang and it ached.
I took pills.
I drank coffee.
I slept on my couch
and my head ached.

Then I ate chocolate and
waited for the sugar.
I thought how this is all new.
I haven't felt any of this.
Haven't breathed like this.
My mind was now apart and
I was scared.
I thought until I forgot
about my headache.

INTERVIEW

"Who died and made you king?" A question I can't stand. I know it's hyperbole but if the scenario were true, the answer would obvious: the King. When I don't reply, he follows it up with, "What makes you so special?" He picks up his coffee mug with two hands which I also can't stand. It reminds me of every coffee commercial on television where the content morning person watches something unfold out his or her kitchen window, holding their mug with two hands and smiling like everything's going to be okay. Everything's not going to be okay. I shake my head at him as if this whole conversation is boring me.

"Why do you think you are so angry?"

"I'm not angry," I say while shaking my head and breathing out a soft laugh, a gesture that's meant to make him feel too old to understand me. And he is too old. He's so old he gets away with poking people in the chest with his index finger when he speaks. He laughs and he pokes, his veiny, wrinkly appendage stretched out at me. He chuckles and pokes.

"Can I ask you something?" I want to respond that he's constantly asking me somethings, why would he need permission now? Why would he stop and ask permission to do what he's already doing? Instead, I close my eyes before I roll them. I feel like being rude, but I don't want him to see.

"Of course."

"Do you think the world owes you something?" I slump half my body to the side and wait a few seconds before answering.

"No. It's not that. I guess I'm just mad. It's not about what they do *to* me, it's about how they *are*."

"Who?"

"...Everyone. The people on the subways. The advertisers. Both of them. Equally. With their slang. With their pandering to how superficial they are. *They* being the people. Their need to be relevant and up to date. Words spelled wrong on purpose, plus-size models, and androgyny. They don't care about these causes. It's just hip. It's cool right now. It's whatever makes them feel adequately liberal or accepting as if those convictions are styles. Accepting is the new pretty. They know to laugh before the joke. They know to clap before the justice. They know it's their favorite movie on their way into the theatre. Groupthink. Like when people say 'all the feels' or that someone 'won' Halloween, or that there is a new skirt for men to wear 'because, fashion.' They can no longer think for themselves or create a sentence or a phrase based on language they know and relate that to their feelings. Social media feeds them information they don't need and mouthfucks their language as well. The ad campaigns feed them too, feed them these conditions. They do it on the subways. *They* being the advertisers. It's that, and it's their telling them what makes them 'real New Yorkers.'" I suddenly realize I've long since let go. My voice is getting louder throughout my rant and I'm moving forward in my seat. He just nods.

"I'm having trouble following. Is it the advertisers or the consumers that bother you? Or both?" He doesn't give me an opportunity to answer and nods himself at the word "both," closing his eyes and moving forward in his chair while he does so, confirming his own words to himself. "Do those ad campaigns make you feel less like a real New Yorker. Is that it?"

"What?..." Now I have the confidence to act rude. "What are you talking about?" He holds out both palms at me, silently asking me to hear him out.

"What do you think makes someone a real New Yorker?"

I pause for a minute, trying to think of a practical answer, then I become impatient.

"I don't know, man. That's a dumb question. I guess you're a real New Yorker when you tell somebody to shut the fuck up and stop analyzing where I'm from." He snickered at this.

"That's fair. So, is that what's got you upset? The perception of New York? The yuppies? The trendys? It's all phony to you?"

"I guess so. I wouldn't say I'm upset. I'm rightfully annoyed by it. You make me sound like I am some Holden Caulfield type. I'm not just anti-trend. I dislike people who are anti-trend more than I dislike the trendy." The old man looked at me blankly.

"You've lost me. Why's that? That makes it seem like you dislike everyone."

"Maybe I do dislike everyone. Do you never feel confused about what annoys you?"

"I didn't say that. It's possible I do feel that way, but we're not talking about me. Can you give me another example, help me see if I understand?"

"Sure," I said too quickly and too loud. The aloofness I was trying to maintain was running out on me. I couldn't keep up. "Like, I'm not sure who I dislike more, the top one percent or people who complain about the top one percent. It's like, get a fuckin' job. Save your money. But that top one percent, well that's just obvious why I dislike them, right? How can you live that way when so many have so little?" I couldn't slow down now. I was hearing the words after they

104

were across the table. "White people...what's worse, white people or people who are constantly complaining about white people? My ex. She has contacted me only one time since she left, and she told me she hopes I am writing. I am writing. Then I read that and want to stop. But I know I should be. But then, am I writing for her or not? I'm not. But how can she know that? She can't. It's not so black and white. And that's another thing, people who think things are black and white. Like, transgender bathrooms or gun control or the registration of sex offenders. Terrorism. It's all subjective. Case sensitive. But then again, I hate when people argue about these things. About...issues. Are you getting this?" I was panting. He sat across from me wearing a slight grin. He used his arm to lift his right leg off his left leg and used his other arm to drape his left leg over his right one.

"Earlier, I asked you if you thought the world owed you something. You didn't answer. Do you?"

"Do I!?" I ejected from my seat. I was standing over him now. "Me!? I worked for years as a waiter. The amount of disrespect...and then again in retail. The amount of people thinking they were better than me on a day-to-day basis, looking at me as if I was dirt." I was shouting now and out of the corner of my eye, I caught a glimpse of my hand. It was shaking. "Even now, do you know what I do for cash? I walk dogs." I couldn't stop myself. "And doormen...doormen. Being so nice to the tenants, but then to me... To me? Like I am dirt, fucking trash. Who do they think they are?"

"Please," he said, leaning forward in his chair. If he poked at me from across the table I swore I was going to rip his finger off. "Please, calm down." I sat back down. I could feel how red my face was. I was still shaking a little bit. "I only have one more question for you, but it's important. Try and think hard before you answer it." I nodded, feeling that if I spoke I would scream. "When was the first time you remember being this angry?"

I sat there across from him for a few long minutes. Nothing was coming to mind at first but then I got it. The thought didn't bring me back into a rage. It came up from inside me calmly. The words came out depleted. There was no engine behind it. It was as if I was paddling along toward the words.

"My mother. It was with my mother."

"Okay, great. Explain it to me."

"Toaster Strudels. Ya know, the kind where the icing comes in separate packets?" He nodded. "My neighbor's mom used to get them. I asked my mother over and over. And every time, Pop-Tarts. Fuckin' Pop-Tarts. I pleaded. I begged. I yelled. I did extra chores. Every time,

Pop-Tarts. I asked her why. No answer. I checked the price. It wasn't much more. I checked the sugar. More or less the same." I felt a tear running down my face. I didn't wipe it, I didn't want to bring attention to it. "Was it just because I wanted them?" My voice was breaking. I was fucking crying now. The words were being chopped up with the inhaling and exhaling. I sounded like a child. I wiped my face and took a big deep breath in. "Okay. I'm done with that. I don't want to talk about that anymore."

He sat there with his old face smiling. He was smiling so big that it closed his eyes.

"Okay. That's fine. I have no more questions for you." He bowed from his seat. "Do you have any questions for me before you go?" I took a shallow breath and surveyed the room.

"Yeah, sure. Did I get it?"

"We will be in touch. You will hear from us by next week either way."

"Thank you very much," I said while rising from my seat and extending my hand to him. He leaned forward, remaining seated. We shook hands. I walked out.

DREAM'S FREE FORM

Love from
the ruptured, mean soil of
my dream's free form.
You ask me, God,
to choose between what
calms my heart
and what makes it bust,
break. Trust?
How can you ask me, God,
to form arteries around metal and
prod at the wounds and feel
my blues, like the flame inside a
combustible vestibule?
God, I've come around
long enough
to be pretty sure You won't
be happy
until You watch it all burn?

MY PERFECT WORLD IDEA

It's always all the time.
The train crawls toward the outside of the tunnel
while being held by the train's dispatcher,
together.
The skyline waited for me
to pitch my perfect world idea
that starts and ends with, "This has all happened before."
The steam escapes the pavement
no different
from the carbon coming star-bound off her eyes.
I guess this isn't what keeps me up at night.
It's not the other side.
Not the broken mother crying,
crying that she can't fix what she so righteously broke.
My disease waits inside my own brain,
awoken when I'm broken up.
And long before, swirling around like a bat
like he never left,
like it will be different this time.
You know. Like when the fireworks break open or when we're on the
water and we can disconnect.
We can run away,
just you and me.
He waits like he never left.
He waits like he's resting.
We can run away,
just you and me.
Now can you imagine the same horizon
on a different timeline.
This is all happening
all the time.

THE WAY

Life keeps going.
You will not outrun this shit.
It will catch up each step of
the way.
You never really leave where you
grew up.

Not only
do I want to keep living,
I'd like to be
thin
with the sex appeal of a Ferris wheel
in a skyline.

There is an ancient time.
Peace
please.
The arguing will only leave you
wanting more.
You'll always find the philosophy
you are looking for.

PATIO

There's nothing sexier than a cigarette.
Nothing hotter on the internet.
All the moving grounds,
softened clouds, and stimulating
ethernet.
A stranger puts her hair up on a park bench.
I feel like I haven't seen New York yet.
If I jump off,
I believe
I'll fly.
"Motherfucker, you wanna bet?"
She walked from here to west Portland
and learned
there's nothing sexier than the girls
you haven't met yet.

HOPE.

You didn't know I'd fall in love with these torn pieces of paper.
The song from last year reminds me of a time that doesn't exist,
a feeling of misguided nostalgia from a summer heat that lives
between the corners of my memory and my imagination.
All that's certain is that I was alone
and I was sad.
But the notes remind me that I was filled with hope.
I keep trading in hope for lovers.
Even already, I find the crossed legs of strange women patiently
waiting to destroy all that's inside me.
And it's not much.
At night, there's screaming in my own head the dark reality that this
might not work out for me.
The soundless pitches and vibrating hell of alone. The
Horror Of Pining for Everyone.

SLAP NIGHT

"He slapped you? Like, in the face?" Tessa asks, putting her hand over her mouth, looking around, and realizing how loud she's said it. Her friend looks around too, embarrassed, and leans in. It looks like she tells Tessa to shut up, but I can't hear from the other side of the bar. There are no other customers left and I start to make myself a vodka and soda while I put away a fruit caddy. They are now whispering to each other and I wonder what they are talking about. They are laughing and are both flushed red. I try not to be nosey, but I am wondering about the slap comment. I walk over to the far corner of the bar where they're sitting and ask what's so funny.

"Oh my God, Tessa, I hate you. I don't even know him, he's going to think I'm crazy," the friend says before I take that moment to introduce myself.

"I'm Jules," the friend replies. We shake hands over the bar. "I work with Tessa."

"Did I not introduce you two?" Tessa says, sounding tipsy. "I'm sorry, I'm the worst. I close the bar down like three nights a week and he lets me stay after hours because I'm *so cool.* Hey, can I smoke in here?"

"Let me lock the doors." I step out from behind the bar and walk across the room to the front door, put in the key, and lock it. It's starting to rain outside. "All good to smoke. So, what's this about getting slapped?" I say as I walk back towards the girls. They are sitting at the end of the bar on the farthest stools away from the front door. I grab an empty stool and bring it behind the bar to sit across from them.

Tessa and Jules couldn't look less alike. Tessa is tall and skinny, her clothes hang loosely off her body. She is blond and has a flat chest and blue eyes. She walked into the bar wearing a black cocktail dress, but went into the stall and changed into her nightly white t-shirt with no bra and her high-cut jean shorts. I always enjoy how she sits at the bar with her feet up on the front of the stool, legs crossed, knees leaning on the bar. Jules is short and thick and has brown hair with hazel eyes. She is wearing a black and blue three-piece getup of a long-sleeve, low-cut shirt that exposes her breasts, a skirt, and knee socks. All are too tight. She has black lipstick that is slightly messed up from drinking out of her pint glass.

"I don't even know him. He's going to think I'm crazy," Jules repeats, looking at Tessa like I'm not sitting in front of them. I stand up and grab the bottle of Jameson and three rocks glasses and start pouring us shots.

111

"I told you, he doesn't care, Jules. It's interesting. Honestly, I think it's kind of hot." Tessa gives us both comically provocative looks.

"I mean, you don't have to tell me if you don't want to," I say, trying to diffuse the awkward moment. Tessa frowns at me. I raise my shot glass and the girls join me.

"Okay, fine. But I just want you to know I don't do shit like this often. This is new to me." As she speaks she is looking back and forth from me to Tessa. "So last night I went to this after-hours party, I guess you can call it, at Hill's Tavern."

"Yeah. I know Hill's. I pass it all the time on my way home."

"And I'm closing the bar down or whatever. And there is this weird guy kind of just sitting there looking at me. He looks, like, Armenian or something. Anyway, we start talking and he is friends with the bartender, this girl Jenny. And he tells me that they have this, like, slap night in the basement of the bar on Monday nights after Hill's closes."

"A slap night?"

"Yeah. So he describes it to me, and it's basically a bunch of them just slapping each other."

"How many people were there?" Tessa asks.

"Like, seven or eight. I mean, I would have been more freaked out, but I know Jenny and she's pretty cool. So I told the dude I would just watch. Anyway, I go down into the basement of the bar with these people and it's exactly that. They take turns kneeling in the middle of the room, slapping each other!"

" Hard?" Tessa turns completely towards Jules, having a tough time with it.

"Surprisingly, yeah. But it was weird. They were, like, loving it."

"Did you try it?" I was only partially sitting on my stool now, one of my legs on the ground.

"Yeah. I mean, I felt I had to."

"And..."

"Honestly, guys." She pauses for a moment. "I have never been so turned on in my life." Tessa lets out a high-pitched laugh, almost like a scream, and puts both hands over her mouth. "I don't know how to describe it. It was like a rush. I got it." I start to picture the scene—Jules kneeling in a dank room, the smell of kegs and garbage, getting slapped. My breathing starts to slow and my heart rate grows.

"So, it was a sexual thing?" I say, sounding like a composed, mature guy who is getting no thrill from this story.

"Yeah. I mean...I went back to the Armenian guy's place." Jules and Tessa share a look that makes me feel left out. "I felt I had to. And

112

gross. Ugh. Afterwards, I was like, *what am I doing here?* But in that moment, I don't know. Oh my God. You must think I am so weird." Jules takes a drink from her glass and spills a drop on her chest. I focus on it, unable to stop. All I can do is shake my head no.

"How do you find yourself in these situations, girl? You are so liberated. I hate you. I would never be able to try anything cool like that." Tessa has this routine of self-deprecation after a few drinks. Lately (although she acts like it's been forever, a common trait of a new regular), she's been shutting down the bar with me a few nights a week and the self-pity is getting old. Jules excuses herself to use the bathroom.

"When I get back, you two better have found something else to talk about. Something personal about one of you maybe?" I watch her walk to the bathroom. I watch her hair brush the small of her back. I focus on the lines in her outfit—where the socks meet the skirt, and the skirt the top. I find an exhilaration in her symmetry.

"Jules is awesome." Tessa can see I'm watching her. "How is Lila?" Lila's name breaks my gaze like a splash of cold water to the face.

"She's great. She's good. At home." I don't say anything else and start to clean the rest of the bar.

For the next forty-five minutes, I clean and drink. I can't take my mind off Jules' story. Tessa has her phone plugged into the audio jack and plays some Arctic Monkeys. The two of them talk about work and their managers and regulars. Their conversation sounds like white noise to me. I pour myself more shots than I usually would while I clean. I keep finding myself looking at Jules—her smeared black lips, her half-exposed chest, the backs of her arms, and her neck as she pulls her hair into a ponytail. I feel myself staring and I feel Tessa watching me. I don't stop looking. I can't tell if Jules can tell. I pour us three more shots once I'm done cleaning.

"Okay, guys. You got me drunk. I need to get home. I have class before work tomorrow," Jules says while Tessa nods as if she also wants to leave and finishes her glass.

"Want to share a cab?" Tessa asks Jules as she puts money on the bar. I push it back to her. "Oh, fuckin' stop, dude. Take it. Please." I leave the cash sitting on the bar for now.

"It was nice to meet you." Jules' hand is facing up, hanging above the bar. I shake it. It's clammy and cold. My eyes dart, meeting hers only for a second, and then move about the room.

"You too, Jules."

Tessa puts her feet on the bottom rung of the stool and leans over the bar to hug me. They walk out and I watch them get into a cab.

113

I change the music and pour myself another shot and a cider. The bar is completely shut down at this point. All that's left to do is unplug my phone, turn off the soundboard, and walk out. I sit in the dark bar and think about Jules. Not in a typical sense, but in a very specific scenario. From where I am sitting at the bar, I can see down the trapdoor into the basement, down into the boiler room. A scene plays out in my mind. She's kneeling down, placing her hands, palms facing up, between the insides of her thighs and her calves. I stand over her and tilt her head back as she pushes her chest up. I stand there for a moment, breathing heavily. I wind my arm back and lean forward. Then it's over. I can't picture the actual slap. It doesn't come to me. I snap out of it and find myself back upstairs sitting alone in the bar.

I leave the bar. It's raining now like it only does in the middle of the night. On the cab ride home, I keep the window half open, close my eyes, and listen to the tires slash against the wet concrete, a consistent sound of small waves crashing but never receding. The cab passes Hill's Tavern and I check to see if there are any lights still on. When I get into my apartment, I have to be quiet. I knock over a glass in the kitchen and it breaks on the floor. I pause for a few seconds to see if Lila wakes up. I assume she did. I will probably hear about it tomorrow.

When I wake up, I am in the guest room, the office, the back room, whatever. It's a glorified closet with a second-hand desk and an uncomfortable futon. It takes me a few seconds to realize I'm there and not in my bed. I often pass out back here to avoid waking up Lila. I have put up blackout curtains that she hates, but that make it easier for me to sleep in. I am overcome by an all-encompassing hangover. I can hear my head pounding against my skull. I once read that the reason you get headaches when you drink is because your brain dehydrates and shrinks causing your brain to knock against your skull. I believe it at the moment. I reach my arm down to the floor to see if I was conscious enough to bring in a glass of water. I was. I chug the water. I feel it seep into my brain like a sponge, expanding it. I put my head back down on the pillow and gasp at the air. My mouth is already dry. I am too tired to get up but too uncomfortable to sleep.

Stuck in this limbo, I take the only action I know will help. I put my hands down the front of my boxers and remember Jules: her black lipstick, her tight skirt and knee socks, the spilled beer falling off her chin onto her chest. The image of her bare knees on cold pavement, her head tilted back, and my hand clapping the side of her face. I am not hurting her. Each time I make contact, her mouth hangs open, exhilarated. Her eyes widen and she smiles deviously. I

114

have to stop before finishing. My heart rate is working my hangover like a boxer on a heavy bag. I'm so weak that this amount of exertion has me breathing in through my nose and out through my mouth. I revel in the breathlessness. All of this wears me out and I begin to nod back off, but only for a few minutes. Then the drumming in my head starts again. I repeat all of it, only this time it goes further and I come closer to finishing, but the exhaustion again cuts me short. I go through this routine a number of times, each time getting more specific and imaginative with what I do to her, what she wants me to do to her so badly, only here we are in the basement of my bar, not Hill's, and there are no other people.

This is how I usually cope with my hangovers. Raising my heart rate and dozing back off, playing out scenes involving whatever random girl sat at the bar the night before. Most of the time I forget about the girl after I finish. Sometimes, if my hangover is bad enough and I stay in bed, maybe I will think about the girl again. But by the time I am up and showered, the girl will cease to exist. This isn't happening with Jules. It isn't so much *her* that is on my mind as much as *her story*. My entire fantasy of Jules this morning is accompanied with a dingy basement (in this case, my job's basement) and a specific action.

I have never had any predilections that involve violence before. I am actually pretty tame when it comes to sex. Even when I watch porn, it's mild stuff. As much as I have my morning fantasies, they are usually just vehicles to combat my physical angst. My real sex life has always been, by most standards, normal. I have never had any casual sex. I have never been unfaithful. All my relations have been with women I am in monogamous relationships with and I have only been with two.

This hangover is particularly brutal, so when I am out of the shower I pour myself a whiskey and grab one of Lila's ciders from the fridge. Before I know it, I'm on Tessa's Facebook page and start looking through her pictures to see if there are any of her with Jules. Sure enough, there is a picture of the two of them at a bar taken one night after their shift, both in their uniforms. I click on her profile and friend request her. I am not taking any time to think about why. The request is sent and I shut my computer. I have another couple of whiskeys and take another shower. I am thinking about Jules. Rather, I am thinking about *it*. The slap night. The way it must have felt, for her, for him. I wonder why this is taking such a hold over me.

I don't like to be initiated. It's simple enough. I can start, I can get it going. If it's the other way around, I instantly get my guard up. Even when I would be into it, if Lila starts in on me, I feel a prickly heat on my skin and I get tense, even angry. Lila thinks it's a bigger problem than it is, in my opinion. It's not like we don't have sex. We do. Not as much as we used to, but that's because we've been together so long and have different schedules. When was the last time I slept with Lila? It's been over a month.

I pour myself another drink, taking my hangover into my own hands. It's only been an hour since the request, but I check my Facebook. She's accepted my request. I spend the duration of that beer looking through her photos. None of them do anything for me until I see one of her kneeling in front of her friends at some party. It's enough for me to envision her like that and change the surroundings to the basement of the bar.

I start to have my way with her again in my head. I'm hoping when I finish that most of this yearning will be out of me. I don't like the fact that I'm so turned on by this. I pour myself another beer and look out my living room window down at Broadway and start to reason with myself. People have fetishes. It's fine to have them. I wonder if Lila would be into something like this, but the thought of slapping her immediately makes my stomach turn. My next thought is, *Is slapping a woman like this considered cheating?* I suppose it is if one or both of you is getting some sort of sexual thrill from it. But people don't consider going to a strip club cheating, or watching porn. I pour myself another drink.

It's now 5:30 and Lila will be home in an hour. She'll be angry I've been drinking if she gets herself close enough to my lips to even realize. I've noticed lately she hasn't kissed me hello, so if I can get away without a hello kiss and get her a glass of wine, maybe she won't be able to tell. I'm feeling a bit tipsy, so I'll have to say very little. I find myself back on my computer, back on Facebook. I feel the booze pulling me into impulsivity. My palms are sweaty. I decide to message Jules. My plan is to ask if I can join her next time she goes to the Hill's slap night. It's innocent enough, I assume. I'll ask her not to tell Tessa. With a whiskey film covering my eyes, I speedily type the message saying exactly that in four sentences, then I turn off my computer and put it away. I don't want to look at it anymore. Just sending the message turns me on. I feel restless and aggressive. I feel embarrassed and guilty. I feel excited.

Lila is in a mood, both from work and from looking at me. She can tell I've been drinking at first sight. She swears she isn't mad. "It's your day off or whatever." She "just had a long day" and "wants to be by herself." She mentions my justification with an obvious discontentment, as if the only thing more insufferable than her saying it is me saying it to her. She goes into the back extra room, the room I woke up in, with a bottle of wine and a glass.

When I open my computer, I have one new notification. A message. I receive the message like the ripping off of a Band-Aid. I want to have the information without having to sit through reading it. I pull out the keywords to get a gist, walk over to the fridge, pull out another beer without bothering to pour it into a glass, then reread the message.

It's really nice to hear from you. I woke up so embarrassed today for having blabbed on about my personal shit to you and Tessa. She always talks about how much she loves going there after work, so it's nice that you don't think I'm weird for it or, like, some whore or something. It's cool you are interested in going to one sometime. If you want, I can reach out to my friend who works there and I am sure they would be cool with you going. But, I don't think I want to go back. It's not that I didn't like it. I did. Probably too much. I just don't want to see that guy again. Maybe, if you don't think it's too weird, I can come by the bar some night and we can just talk about it or, I don't know, do something similar? It could be good for both of us. Just let me know. If you aren't into it that's fine. But I hope you are.

I read the message a few times while nursing my beer, the last one in the house. I have the cursor on the line waiting to write back. Her message is perfect. It's also the worst-case scenario. She more than called my bluff. Was this what I wanted? I thought she would get back to me and say that she would be happy to bring me next time she went and leave it at that. Maybe mention talking to her friend that goes. All things I could get out of. But this? She has given me a direct route in. If this is what I want to do, here it is. I look at the screen and rub my chin with one hand and the top of my thigh with the other. I could just not answer. If I want out now, that's my only move. If I want in—it's right there.

Lila walks out of the back room. I quickly minimize the window. She doesn't even look my way and walks into the bedroom. She must have finished the wine and fallen asleep on the futon. I'm glad she woke up on her own and made it into bed. Whenever I let her sleep there overnight, she gets angry that I didn't get her up and into the bedroom. The blackout curtains disorient her, so she says.

I open the window and I type back, *Can you come by the bar tomorrow night around the time I close? I usually close at 2:00 a.m. on weekdays.*

I send the message and Facebook instantly lets me know she is typing back.

Yes.

I can't let myself think about it anymore tonight. I have already finished the last beer, so I grab the whiskey from the cabinet, the nice stuff Lila wants me to save for company, and I take down a final three-finger nightcap, cork the bottle, and put it away. I keep my hand on the wall and walk slowly towards the bedroom, careful not to wake up Lila.

I wake up and Lila is gone to work. The conversation with Jules seems like a distant memory. My head aches and my mouth is dry. I decide this is all crazy and that she probably won't even show up tonight. If she does, I will just give her some free booze and let her stay in the bar and smoke after it's closed. People love that. But this whole slapping business is just insane.

I get to the bar at 3:00 p.m. I am feeling a little sluggish from the night before, so I set the bar up slowly, but quickly enough to be open by four. The bar is a dive. One room, no kitchen, a cracked wooden bar with a matching floor. The bathrooms are worn and permanently dirty no matter how much we clean them. There is a trap door on the floor behind the bar that leads to the basement. At the bottom of the stairs, if you go right there's the office. One desk with a busted swivel chair and papers everywhere. Bottles line the wall as it doubles as a liquor closet. Connected to the office is a walk-in refrigerator, better known as the keg room, and off the other side is a bathroom. If you go left at the bottom of the stairs you will find the furnace room. Stone walls, concrete floor, dripping water from the exposed pipes. That's where I let my friends smoke weed. There are no cameras in the furnace room.

At 4:00, the good ol' boys start showing up. The same ones as every other day. I'm holding onto my notion that today I'm not going to drink. If Jules does show up, I will just tell her I was curious and want to hear more about it, but I am not literally interested in the whole thing. I'm feeling relieved that the curiosity, the arousal, has worn off some.

The shift goes on with the same regulars as always. I make the same conversations I do every day. The rain is still lingering. I have that melancholy one gets after enough days of continuous rain. I'm bored. I check my phone. It's 9:30 and Lila hasn't texted me once today. I shoot her a quick text. I check my phone around 10:00. No reply. As I'm looking at my phone, Kyle walks in. I know Kyle through a friend and we start chatting as soon as he sits down. He is taking down whiskeys and beginning to enjoy the conversation. He likes to get deep, talk politics and religion. I am restless and envious of the fun he is having, so I decide to join him for a shot. I have another. I open a bottle of Magners Cider, open my throat, and swig back half of it.

At 10:30, I check my phone. Two messages. The first is from Lila.

Hi. Long day. Sorry I didn't text you. Home now. Going to go to bed. Please be quiet coming in. XO

I see the other text is from a number I don't have saved, so I mindlessly answer Lila, *XOXO*, then open the other text. *Hey! It's Jules. I got your number off Tessa (don't worry, I just said I had a question about looking for a bartending gig). We still on for tonight? I get done around 12-1 and can jump in a cab and come over after.*

Kyle is talking at my zoned-out face. He doesn't notice I'm not listening because I've become a pro at ignoring customers while looking like I'm listening. My heart is beating, my palms are sweating. Every single intention of throwing this meeting out the window has fled. Every single desire has instantly returned as if flooded in at once. Suddenly, the night is moving too slowly and I can no longer pretend to find Kyle interesting.

When she shows up around 1:00 a.m., my wild fantasy is diluted. She looks so normal in her work clothes with her thick brown hair tied back in a ponytail and wearing a black shirt and black pants, her purse hanging off her shoulder. She gives me that "fuck work" look as she walks past the bar to the far corner where she sat two nights ago.

I make it casual. A napkin on the bar, a drink order, a "How was your shift?" She does the same. "Fuckin' Upper West Siders, shit tips, power-hungry managers." Through it all, a smile made only through eye contact—an expectation. And excitement in our body language—a nervousness in my movements—an impatience in everything I do.

It's raining outside. There are three people at the bar besides Jules. I know two of them will leave when I say last call. The third is Kyle, whom I've let shut down the bar with me and who I can tell has no intention of leaving. Jules sits at the end of the bar looking at her phone, but when she looks up momentarily, I can feel her brief glances. They are violent even though she is calm.

"Last call!" I turn the music back up, but not all the way, and no one budges. I give a five-minute window for ordering the last drinks.

"I'll have another whiskey," Kyle says, picking up on my want to leave, but not respecting it. Lonely bar patrons—either they have nowhere else they want to be, or nowhere else wants them to be there. I pour Kyle his whiskey then turn up the lights. The light eats the flesh off all five of us. I turn to Jules. Her eyes are bloodshot and her face white. I can see the hairs that have escaped her ponytail. For a second, she looks like a ghost. Her disheveled appearance looks wanting like she is ready to pounce up and attack. I can do nothing but grip my bar rag and try to control my breathing.

The two customers get up to leave. I wonder how I'll get rid of Kyle while letting Jules stay. I can't be honest, obviously. What is it to be honest? Kyle knows Lila. It could be worse. It could be any of my other single friends who would have been hitting on Jules, the only other girl at the bar.

"Hey dude, I have to do inventory tonight so..." I am so overzealous I accidentally interrupt something he's saying. "Let's get together soon, man. Some night I'm off." He nods in agreement, mouth full of whiskey. His eyes dart back and forth between me and Jules. She's looking into her phone with a half-empty glass. As he stands up, he looks as if he's going to ask me something, but puts his lips together and scrunches up his chin, giving a disappointed smile that lacks the actual smile part.

The first thing I do is turn the extra lights back off. Kyle is still outside smoking a cigarette and sees them go off. At that, he walks out to the street and hails a cab. Jules has put her phone down. She is looking at me with a seriousness now and I can't tell if she is confused or just anticipating what I'll do next.

"So, listen," I begin in a casual tone, mildly moving my shoulders up then down and slightly tilting my head. "I don't want you to think I'm wei—"

"I don't think we should talk much before," she says matter-of-factly.

Jules sat in that same seat two nights ago bashful, yet tonight she carries an unspoken experience. Her shoulders are square and her head is held high atop her straight neck. I wonder if she is compensating for her own nerves or if I am standing in front of a different version of Jules than I was the other night.

"I also don't think we should wait too long." It isn't until she speaks again that I realize I haven't replied to the first instruction.

"Yeah, you're probably right." My words feel jagged and awkward leaving my mouth like I am learning them as they pass through me. My tongue feels heavy in my mouth. She stands up, takes a step forward, and pauses at the bar. I pick up the wooden slab to let her in behind. My arms feel similar to my tongue. I look down at her short, black heels as they step onto the sticky bar mats. Her body is small and compartmentalized in her work outfit—she is divided into parts: neck, torso, legs. Each is defined and stands apart. She has that

120

light shine from the sweat of working a long shift. I look her up and down, shamelessly now, and I watch her watch me. Then she looks down at the trap door, reminding me to keep the momentum.

I walk in front of her down the steep steps. When we get to the bottom, I go left towards to furnace room and she follows. I turn on the one working light which shines a shade of light green and occasionally flickers. We are both quiet. I can hear myself breathing and wonder if she can hear it too. The rusted pipes drip onto the puddle on the concrete floor. I watch Jules look around at the four cinder block walls, the decrepit pipes, and the furnace which, compiled of old and new parts, looks like a mechanical heart.

My thoughts are a step behind my body. I can't imagine, now that we're here, what the mechanics will be. The sound of my heart beating is blocking out any organized thinking. Jules continues to help me out.

"Okay, you can go first." The word "first" bounces into my head quickly and I decide to throw it out, fearing I will ruin the momentum. She stands directly in front of me, the top of her head just below my chin. "Remember, openhanded. You are not trying to knock my head to the ground. But you need to really slap me. It needs to count. You will fuck this up if you are trying too hard not to hurt me."

All I can do is nod. The urge, the one that has been marinating in me for forty-eight hours is now boiling. It's become a tangible object I cannot live without—an event I cannot wait much longer for. I rub my sweaty hands against my jeans as she kneels on the concrete. She connects her hands behind the small of her back and raises her chin. She makes deliberate eye contact with me, holds it for a moment, then closes her eyes.

I stand over her and think quickly about not holding back, about not ruining this. I raise my hand behind my shoulder, swing it forward, careful not to put much arm into it, and as I get to her face, I let my wrist carry the majority of the force. It echoes around the room. She jilts back and to the side. Her hands come undone and she braces against the floor beside her, stopping herself from falling on her face. She breathes heavy, pulsating breaths, letting her head sway over her chest. She then lifts her head up looking at the ceiling and lets out a satisfied moan. I see the red mark on her face and realize in watching her I have been completely taken out of myself.

I did it. I feel calm and intense—satisfied and strong. Jules starts to get up. She is moving slowly. She catches me off guard when she starts laughing. It almost seems manic. She takes in a long breath through her nose and releases through her mouth. She looks at me very differently than before the slap. Her eyes are erratic and wild now.

"Now it's your turn." When she says this, I want to protest. A flurry of words come to the tip of my tongue and are all stopped there. I stand helpless for a few awkward seconds while Jules sustains her glare. I kneel on the cold floor. I mimic the way she held her hands and a whole new nervousness comes over me. Jules never mentioned her doing any slapping the other night. I hadn't anticipated being on the receiving end, although it makes perfect sense. Why wouldn't it go both ways? I look at her. I wonder if she can see I'm nervous. I don't want her to see that in me. I reluctantly close my eyes. In the pitch black, I hear the dripping of the pipes, the humming of the furnace, and a ringing in my head. It feels like it lasts ages.

The sting. The warmth against my skin. My head jerks to the side. My mouth waters. It takes a moment for it to set in, and when it does, it expands down my shoulders, through my arms, all the way to my fingertips. A staggered heartbeat and an itching perspiration comes over me. My eyes squint and I make two hard fists.

I feel any control over myself evaporate. Before I can take a handle on my body, I am on my feet and my arms are out. I don't even notice what I am doing until I look down and see her feet are not touching the ground. A series of red and yellow lights are blocking my vision. I come to and feel her trying to swallow against my palm. The first noise to come back to me is her gasping. I see her eyes bulging and her body twitching. I notice how much bigger I am than her.

When I let go, she drops to the ground. She is panting and starts to shake. I take a few steps back and catch myself against the furnace. There is about six feet of distance between us now and she looks up at me, all four of her limbs on the concrete. Her eyes are bloodshot. Her face is white.

"I...I'm sorry. I don't—" I hear the words softly bounce around the room, but I'm unsure if I am saying them out loud. She stands up slowly, looks at me one more time and quickly walks out and heads up the stairs. I wait a few moments before following her. When I get up through the trapdoor, I expect to find her gone—exited out the front door of the bar. But she is not gone. She is sitting back on her barstool, fixing her hair, looking into a pocket mirror. I stand there mortified, confused, with remnants of adrenaline still flowing through me.

"Listen, Jules. I didn't know I would do that. I don't know what came over me. I—"

"Don't apologize." Her tone is back to professional. She finishes what's in her glass, stands up, puts her bag around her shoulder, and walks out of the bar. I watch her through the glass front doors. She lights a cigarette and peers at me one time, then she's gone. I'm left alone in the bar. It's never felt so quiet. For the first time in all the years working there, I can hear the hum of the furnace in the basement.

I can't sleep. The booze feels like water on a duck's feathers. I keep going over and over every detail. I keep wondering what I should do next. Should I reach out to her? Should I just pretend it never happened? I don't have to see her again. There is no way she will come back into the bar. Will she tell Tessa? Why did I react that way? I lay on my back, then move to my side, then back on my back, then back over to my other side. Lila eventually sits up. I expect her to ask, "What's up? Is everything okay?" But she just grabs her pillow and walks into the back room. I don't mind. I'm happy to be alone. I decide I need to send Jules a message. I need to just say, "I'm sorry," one more time. I go into my living room and open a curtain. It's 6:30 a.m. and daylight is just starting to peak in. The garbage trucks roar in front of my apartment. I go to my emergency bottle and pour myself a little glass. I take a sip as I open my computer.

One new message: Jules. I can't believe it. I open the message.

Hey. I don't know what happened back there, but I can't sleep. All I can think about is your hands on me. The fear. It's driving me crazy. It's driving me crazy that it's driving me crazy. I'm not mad at you. I think we can help each other. I think we need each other. I need you to push me. Do you work next Wednesday? I want to come back.

I read the message five or six times before responding.

I'll be there.

I shut the computer and get back into bed. I fall into a deep, peaceful sleep.

There are bar shifts filled with mundane small talk and drinking myself to sleep. There is a day off with Lila involving a trip to the farmers market, brunch with her friends, ordering food, and watching a movie together. We even have sex. There is a Sunday off with my friends Eric and Matt. We watch football and order wings—I bet the under and I lose. Nothing is happening in my head except Wednesday night. I check my inbox seven or eight times a day and I reread the message. *I need you to push me.* I wonder what she could mean. I picture it over and over, my coming to, my hands around her neck. While Lila fingers through the kale at the market, I'm staring at the pavement picturing the basement floor of the furnace room. The brunch conversations come to me in fragments. I try to keep up. I'm

123

playing out scenarios. What she could want. What she wants to be pushed towards.

Tuesday night, I wave goodbye to my last customers, a group of German tourists staying in the hotel across the street. I pour myself a whiskey and grab a bottle of Bud. I stand at the entrance of the furnace room and set my drinks down. I flick on the light and sit on the floor. I listen to the dripping of the pipe into the puddle that never gets any bigger and the hum of the furnace. I look like a Buddhist monk or one of the girls who does yoga in the window of the studio on Broadway. I smell mold, but for a second I think I impossibly smell her perfume. I drink. I study the old pipe in the corner that juts out of the ceiling and makes a C down towards the floor and connects to the back wall, it reminds me of an Egyptian statue with its rust-colored physique. It has a beautiful statuesque quality to it I never noticed before.

I don't allow myself to imagine the things I think she means by *push*. Any expectation, any quick excitement makes me feel wrong, makes me second guess what I'm doing, and could make me stop. So when she is sitting in front of me the next night, sipping her drink, I am trying to repress the thoughts of bending her like that pipe, of grabbing her ponytail, her neck, her ankles.

When the last customer walks out, I follow him to the door, locking it behind him. I walk back behind the bar and swing open the trapdoor. *Keep the momentum going.*

"Wait," she says with a playful gaze in my direction bringing light to my zealousness. "Sit with me for a second."

I sit on the stool next to hers trying my best to seem calm and cool.

"What's up?" I catch myself rubbing the tops of my jeans and biting my lip while I wait for her to answer. I put my hands on the bar and take an inconspicuous deep breath hoping to calm my body. She doesn't answer and is looking down, serious now. After a long pause, she turns to me, her eyes filled with tears.

"I've lost feeling."

Not knowing what to say, I go to improvise a response, but before I can get anything out she continues. "And I feel bad for how I'm going to use you. I see what it's like for you. You can't stand it, can you? To be touched?"

"Well, I get a little uncomfortable sometimes, sure, but—"

"That was more than a little uncomfortable. You strangled me." She doesn't seem upset or accusatory in saying the word strangle. She pronounces the word almost softly, but still, it hurts to hear it.

"It was a reflex. To being slapped. I wouldn't do that to someone

124

who just touched me, I'm not crazy." My tone sounds pathetic and timidly defensive.

"It's okay. We can help each other." She puts her hand on top of mine and her other on my bicep. "Let me build you up. Let me touch you. And let it rise in you. Use it back on me. Help me feel."

I look at her, not knowing what to say, not being able to say no, not wanting to. "What happened? Why can't you feel? You can talk to me if you want."

"I could ask you the same thing. But I don't need another therapist or a shoulder to cry on. Do you want to talk to me about what happened to you? Or do you just want to help each other?"

"Should we have, like, a safe word or phrase?" I ask. She looks around the empty bar for a few seconds, her eyes unfocused on anything.

"How about, 'I love you?'"

"I love you?"

"Yeah. It will suck all the fun and excitement out of it, snap us out of it." She raises her eyebrows and the sides of her mouth curl up into a cynical smile.

"I like it."

I sit in the furnace room in an old folding chair taken from the office. Jules pulls my shirt off over my head and takes a headband from her purse and positions it over my eyes. I feel the sweat seep into the headband and I fight the urge to ask what she is doing. And as if reading my mind, she whispers into my ear.

"Trust me. Whatever you feel, try to keep it in. And when you can't anymore, use that."

She stands behind me and I feel her stomach against the back of my head as she leans forward. Her nails begin to dig into the fronts of my shoulders. The rage instantly surfaces but I do as she asks. I push it down. Through the headband, I see a faded green and dark gray. She pulls one of my arms behind the back of the chair and follows that up with the other one. I feel trapped like I'm in a room full of people all making for the exit at once. I feel the hot itch on my skin. She holds my hands together with one hand while she makes her way down my front with the other, pressing her nails against my stomach. Before she makes it down the front of my pants, I am standing. The chair is knocked across the room and the headband is crunched between my fingers. I have somehow brought her to her knees and stand over her. My hand swings back and then forth, remembering to focus the movement of my wrist and not my shoulder. The headband is now in

125

her mouth. My arm continues to swing. I move her to the floor in one motion and as I feel my knee rest on the front of her chest, I hear words muffle through the headband. I take it out of her mouth.

"I...love...you." She is gasping for air between each word.

That's how it goes. Every week she comes by on Wednesday nights and we *play* our game. It's a progressive art. It takes more and more to fill me up and more and more to bring her out, to make her feel. We use ties, we use hot water and ice. I spend my week coming up with new ways to use her, or as she would say, to help her, and she does the same. The only thing it seems we don't do are the standard showings of affection. We never kiss, we never do any sexual acts, we don't cuddle or hug, and most importantly, we don't talk afterward. Usually, she will tell me she loves me, announcing the end, then we will head up to the bar and silently have a drink and smoke a cigarette.

There are some hoops we have to jump through. Tessa, for one, who works with Jules and comes into the bar almost every night. I start to tell her I need to do inventory on Wednesdays after the shift ends and Jules hangs out at the wine bar around the corner until we are sure she's gone. One night, my boss comes into the bar while we are downstairs. Luckily, I hear him and shut the door to the furnace room and sit in the office. He's just by to grab some tools he left at the bar that he needs to work on his house and wants to avoid traffic by coming into the city in the middle of the night. It ruins our ritual for the week, but only adds a build up to the following week's meeting.

Our biggest obstacle by far is the building of tolerance to the acts. No matter how hard we try and push it without hurting each other seriously, no matter how much something works, it is stale by the following week. Maybe some thrills last over and over, but when the objective is losing oneself and the fear of being out of control, redundancy just kills it. It takes more and more to build me up, to help her. And I can't fake it. With something like this, something that involves real fear and real anger, it's a lot like losing weight or finding God—you get what you put into it. Sometimes we need to restart, and sometimes it just doesn't work at all, but when it does, there is an unparalleled feeling of being lost that can only be blocked by those three words—I love you—they bring me back to life. They quell my anger. They make me sad.

She has found a way to genuinely bring out a physical rage in me, but it's not that simple. I have to know she is enjoying it. That has to be the reality and I can only stay in that reality by the distant glint in her eye while we *play*. I don't explain this to Jules. When we sit at the bar afterward, quietly nursing our drinks and smoking, I never tell her that I see a gratefulness, even a joy in her eyes the whole time. I'm afraid if I do, it will ruin it for both of us.

I walk into my apartment. It's 5:00 a.m. and I am surprised to see Lila sitting up in the kitchen with half a glass of red wine. It's her weekend and I wonder if she was out with her friends and has recently come home. Her face is flushed and her hair's a mess. She is wearing a white tank top and workout shorts.

"I didn't expect to see you up."

"I couldn't sleep. I feel like I haven't seen you in weeks." It looks like she has been crying or is just half awake. "I thought you would be home earlier than this."

"Inventory." I am a little drunk and wiped out. My sessions with Jules always leave me exhausted and usually I come home and lay on my couch and go over the details of the way I have just distorted her body, the red marks, and the guttural sounds she emitted and take care of myself. But tonight here is Lila, and she is right. I haven't seen her one on one in a while. I walk over to her and I stand between her legs. I take my hand, which is still red and hot from my time with Jules, and I put it on her cheek. I kiss her and I feel at home. I feel safe. I pick her up and move her over to the couch where we are together, and I notice how gentle I am being with her. It is sensual and relaxed. I haven't felt this comfortable with her in years.

When we are done, we move into the bedroom. The sun is coming up now and I don't bother showering. She gets in bed while I brush my teeth and even though she is awake, I get into bed quietly. I don't know if it's just by habit or if the morning sun is giving off an impression of softness. I lay on my side and she reaches her arms around me and holds me. She knows I hate this—the breath on the back of my neck, her arms dangling loosely over my torso. I bear it for longer than I usually do before I turn around, turn her around, and spoon her from behind.

What is it to be scared? Is it fear of pain? Or simply fear of the unknown? Is it fear that's helping Jules feel? I often want to ask what took her feeling away, what happened. I think about that first night at the bar, the night she sat with Tessa and giggled about the slap night at Hill's Tavern like a schoolgirl talking about a crush. That glint in her eye, the one that shines through when she is bound on the furnace room floor, looking up at me. It was there in that conversation. I see it clearly, and it makes me pity her.

It doesn't work tonight. I get annoyed at her attempts to provoke me. I get annoyed but not violent, and a few times I try to fake it, but she sees right through me. She tries something new, something she thinks will be humiliating to me, and I throw her to the floor. Her head bounces off the concrete and as she turns to look up at me, she must see that I am concerned.

"I knew this would happen," she says while slowly propping herself up. "You've lost it. I knew you would."

"Maybe tonight just isn't the night, Jules."

"Ha!" A sarcastic laugh. "It's not just tonight. You're getting soft. You'd probably rather be with your girlfriend watching Netflix or something. Typical." She is gathering her belongings and starts walking towards the basement steps. "This isn't working because you're a pussy," she says, looking back over her shoulder. "You're weak. You don't scare me—I can't get a thrill out of a guy like you." She makes her way up the stairs.

I take three swift strides towards the stairs and grab the back of her ponytail. I pull her back down. She lets out a loud breath and drops her stuff. I turn her around and see that stupid look of excitement on her face. It makes me repulsed instead of angry. I turn her back around and feel in her weight how she is letting me. It's just part of her game. I grab the zip ties the bar sometimes uses for recycling and nudge her towards the corner of the furnace room. I press her back up against the big, rusty, C-shaped pipe in the corner. The one that looks like an Egyptian statue. I pull her hands over her head and extend them behind the pipe and I tie them together. I tie another one around her waist and the rusty, damp metal. I move behind the pipe and straddle it, grabbing her ankles with each of my hands, and I tie them together. She's now hog-tied to the pipe. I turn around and look at her. She has that look, that look like she's trying to look scared, but knows this is role play. I grab her throat and give it a light, playful squeeze. Then I walk out. I shut the furnace room door behind me and I walk up into the bar.

I pour myself a whiskey and I grab a bottle of Bud. I sit down and turn on one of the TVs. Knowing she is down there gives me this thrill. There's a percussion to my heartbeat as I sit and watch baseball highlights. I have a second round and a third until I am good and tipsy, until I almost, in a subconscious way, forget she is there. I smoke a cigarette. Would a pussy leave someone tied up in a basement?

Over an hour later, I walk into the furnace room and she looks like a figurehead off the bow of a boat. Her arms, waist, and ankles are tied to the pipe, but her head is dangling forward, her hair covering her face. I walk over and untie her ankles, then her waist, and finally her

128

arms. She drops to her knees and looks up at me. She looks exhausted and dismayed. Her face is shades of red and white. I notice there are marks from the rusty pipe on her back.

"I didn't say, 'I love you.'"

There is usually a pause when Lila asks me if I want to go to a museum with her or to one of her friends' experimental art films, but today when she asks, I squint my eyes, smile, and nod in agreement. I want to go. I stand by her on the sidewalk. We hold hands. The fact that I had a girl tied up in the bar's basement last night is not pushed aside. On the contrary, it's forefront in my mind. My aggression is down in the furnace room, at least for now.

Like everything else with Jules, they are all temporary fixes and the real brunt of my discontentment is taken out on Lila—but taken out much differently. The idea of being physically violent to Lila makes my stomach turn, but I find other ways to punish her. I will stay at the bar below our apartment and turn off my phone knowing she is expecting me home, making her take the walk down to get me, a walk I know she hates making. I'll make messes and leave messes. I will call out her friends and start arguments with them about politics or religion. I will grow annoyed by almost everything about her, just wanting to feel the way I do when I am leaving the furnace room. The more aggression I can leave in the furnace room, the better.

When Lila tells me her mother is coming for the weekend, I know I must find a way to bring out the most patient version of myself. Her mother doesn't like me, I know that. She thinks I'm a drunk. Every time she visits, she gets in Lila's head and for the weeks to follow, Lila becomes distant. I know she tells her to leave me and I know she comments about every impatient or aggressive move I make, no matter how small or insignificant they are. But this time, not only will I come off normal, I'll come off loving and kind. I know it. I tell my boss I need the weekend off, Friday through Sunday, and I invite Jules to the bar on Thursday night.

As she stands in front of me, I can tell she is excited about whatever trick she had conjured up to ignite me. My shift is long, filled with difficult customers and shitty tips. On top of that, I have to find a way to get both Kyle and Tessa out of the bar without using the inventory excuse since it isn't Wednesday. I'm tired and just the sight of Jules standing in the doorway of the furnace room has my heart thumping not nervously, but contemptuously.

"So, I was thinking," she begins in a casual tone. But before she can finish her thought, I have taken the two strides across the room and have her in my grip. Her eyes widen with shock. Holding her neck, I let her eyes meet mine and she sees there is no need to set me off. I'm there. I turn her head away from me. I don't feel like looking at her anymore. I drag her over to the Egyptian statue pipe and fasten her to it. The door of the furnace room slams behind me. I pull out the keys to the room, the ones I had picked up from the super before my shift, lock the door, and leave.

I walk around Central Park absorbing Lila's mother's stories. The leaves are blooming and the colors seem so bright after the long winter. She goes on about April in New York and I'm not sickened by her. Or if I am, I don't care that I am. Lila's hand is in mine and it is moving about. She seems anxious, but I chalk it up to her expecting me to say something snarky to her mother. But it won't happen. I feel at peace and as we discuss dinner plans, I smile and nod at each suggestion. Lila smiles at me, trying to hide her nervousness, and I want to tell her it won't happen this weekend. I won't be getting drunk. I won't be arguing with her mother. It will be a nice weekend.

At dinner, I think about whether I'll stop by the bar and check on Jules. I decide against it. The concern and compassion could be the wrench in the system. I try to not think about her wellbeing for the same reasons. But at lunch the following day, I am struck with a moment of panic. Panic about what will happen to me if something goes wrong, if she isn't okay. I excuse myself after the meal and head over to the bar.

It's busy—crowded with day drinkers. The front glass doors are open and the sun is shining in. My friend Alex is bartending and is surprised to see me. I tell him the owner has called me to check on something in the furnace room and to keep going about his business. I unlock the door and the dark sticks itself out to meet me. I switch on the half-broken lights and walk over to her. I hear the water dripping and the hum of the pipes. As I get closer, I hear her breathing slowly. I stand in front of her and pull the headband from her mouth. Her eyes are bloodshot and her mouth is dry. She looks at me with a ferocity I haven't seen before. I feel a mixture of pride at how far I have taken it, but concern for her health. The latter gets the best of me.

"I can't stay. If you want me to take you down, say the words." She looks at me, zero change in her emotion. I have a water bottle in my hand and I pour a little in her mouth. It wets her lips and then overflows slowly over her bottom lip. She blinks at me. She says nothing. I place my hand softly on the top of her head while I put the headband back in her mouth.

Before I leave, something peculiar catches my eye. On her back, where she is pinned against the pipe, rust has spread all over her white shirt. I chalk it up to the dampness and think nothing of it. I walk out, turning off the light, and lock the door behind me.

The rest of the weekend goes on smoothly. Lila's mother even gives me a rare hug before she leaves, holding on tight for a number of seconds, something she's never done before. Lila always gets emotional when saying goodbye to her mother and I am here for her. I am proud of myself.

That night, we drink wine silently in the living room. I know Lila is upset about her mother and instead of antagonizing her, I give her some space. We watch reruns of shows she likes even though every time I look over at her she is staring out the window. I don't switch to something I'd rather watch. I just sip my wine and place my hand on her leg. She turns to me and forces out a smile. I'm almost sad that she is upset about her mother leaving. We go into the bedroom at the same time. She has on her sweats and has washed her face. I lay down with her and she kisses me goodnight. As I lay there next to her in the dark, I think about Jules. I imagine her shallow, sparse breaths from the afternoon before and try to match them. As I am starting to drift off, Lila turns and puts her arms around my waist. Her warms breath beats against the side of my neck. I fall asleep with her up against me.

When I open the door to the furnace room and flip the switch, the back wall lights up like a movie screen and starts flashing on and off. The overhead light fixture has broken and is swaying in the middle of the room, facing the back wall. Through the flashing I can, if only barely, make out the shape of Jules against the pipe coming in and out of view. I slowly walk towards her, making sure to avoid the swaying, flickering fixture. Standing in front of her, I am overcome with what I see. Or rather, what I don't see. Her form is in front of me, but not her body. The ties, all still in place, have not been moved or untied since I tied them. The pipe illuminates a more prominent gold in the sparse greenish flashes. I look closely and inspect the pipe. I run my hand up and down it and I feel her curves along the moist metal surface. I pull out my phone and turn on the flashlight. A wave of horror engulfs me as I see her face, molten and metallic. The headband, still in her mouth, has an alloy bridge over the middle of it and I try to pull it out, but can't. The body and legs are fused so well that if it wasn't for the outline of her eyes, the holes of her nose, and the hardened material stuck where her mouth was, she would be unnoticeable. I turn off the flashlight and as I walked past her, I see her damp tennis shoes, placed toe tips

131

down on the floor, to either side of the pipe, like they have simply slid off. I grab them and take them upstairs with me. After disposing of the shoes in the trash can in the corner, I open the bar.

It's a sunny, mild spring day. Teachers and construction workers join the regulars. It seems everyone is in a pleasant mood. Surprisingly, the shift moves on quickly. Each hour I walk down and check on Jules. I check on the pipe. I let myself become stricken with fear and then laugh at myself for falling for what has to be an elaborate prank. I stand behind the bar and marvel at how she's pulled this off. She must have involved a locksmith and a welder. Just having that thought, really thinking out what it must have taken to pull it off, sends me back into a restrained hysteria.

Around midnight, I think about her purse. She put it down in my office before we went into the furnace room on Thursday. It's there. Her cell is dead. Her wallet, equipped with her ID, credit cards, and $215 in tip money. The sight of it sends me striding back into the furnace room. When I switch on the light, a violent spark shoots out. The bright white debris from the light simmers on the dank, constant puddle. I open my flashlight and reexamine her. It? Her face is less recognizable than earlier, mostly all metal. If this was some sort of weld job, art thing, it wouldn't change.

I stuff her purse in my bookbag. Although the bar's security system hasn't recorded in over three years, I take the faulty tape out. I return behind the bar to find an impatient regular, Eddie, waving his empty pint glass waiting for a refill, and Kyle, sitting, pretending to be patient.

"Kyle. What's up, man?" I pour the refill for Eddie.

"You okay, man? You seem flustered."

"Oh yeah. Fine. Just organizing some things down in my office." I pour a whiskey for him and one for me.

"I was about to help myself, dude." He laughs at his own joke.

I stand nervously behind the bar, looking out the glass doors at the rain while Kyle talks endlessly about what is going on with him. I feel I do a fantastic job at making it sound like I am listening while not listening at all. I have been bartending so long I know when to add a, "Yeah," "Sure," "Okay," just by one's inflection.

I continue to play out the likely and unlikely scenarios in my head. Options go from ridiculous to all too real and back again like a game of Pong. I wonder if she is dead, and if so, did I murder her? Do I crack open the pipe? With what? That's a main line in the building and if she is indeed in there, she is dead and the destruction of the pipe will set off an alarm on the whole building and I'll be found out. But then again, people don't turn into metal. I was no honors science student, but I know that much. Another idea that pops in and out of my brain is my own sanity, but that rabbit hole is too overwhelming.

I don't want to be here anymore. I want to be home with Lila, warm in our bed. If by some unexplainable means Jules is now forever in the furnace room, then I should be safe—my aggressions and urges trapped down there with her. Eddie finishes up and I curtly tell Kyle that I can't hang around tonight. I need to get home to Lila. He is a little taken aback but that's the least of my concerns.

As I am putting my last touches on my closing routines, I tell Kyle he can stay and walk out with me. As I finish, Tessa walks up to the locked front door holding her bag over her head until she's under the awning and knocks. I grab my bag, filled with Jules' belongings, and turn off the light. I tap Kyle on the shoulder as I walk past him towards the doors. "Come on, man. We're walking out." He throws back the last of what's in his glass. I meet Tessa at the front door after letting Kyle walk out in front of me. While I'm locking the door behind me, Tessa acknowledges how I have failed to acknowledge her.

"Uh, hi. Closing a little early tonight?"

"Yeah, Tess, sorry. Need to get home early tonight."

"Well, I wasn't coming by to drink anyway." She scoffs defensively. "Have you seen Jules?" The sound of her name sends a shiver down my spine.

"Um, no. Why?" It takes me a second to find my voice and I wonder if she notices. Kyle stands to the side of us, his head bouncing back and forth to whomever is speaking.

"She hasn't been at work in two days and nobody can get ahold of her. I'm getting fucking worried." She looks worried.

"Yeah, dude. Haven't seen her." I see Kyle looking like he wants to ask some questions, but I have filled up his glass so many times tonight without charging him a dime, that he knows his words will slur and he doesn't want to show that to Tessa.

"Well, okay then. If she comes by or whatever, call me, I guess." She says this as I walk past her, towards the street and put my hand out. A cab almost immediately veers towards me.

"Got it." I can feel how casual I look, and I am proud of myself.

Walking up the stairs to my apartment, I hear commotion below at the bar. There is a decent crowd in there for a rainy Monday, but the rush has come and gone and on any other night I would stop in for a couple. I reach into my bag. I feel her purse rub against the side of my arm while I fish for my keys at the bottom. Right as I get ahold of them, my apartment door opens. Standing, taking up the majority of the frame, is Lila's brother, Tomas. He looks serious.

"What are you doing here?" I don't mean to sound so obviously annoyed, but I can't help it.

"Listen. You can't stay here tonight. Come back tomorrow afternoon. We'll be all done." I look past him and see one of Lila's friends and then another. All the lights are on. I see boxes everywhere and our belongings moved around. I don't see Lila.

"Where is Lila, Tomas?"

"She doesn't want to see you. Don't make this more difficult than it has to be."

I look him up and down. He is a bigger guy than I am, there is no use in trying to get physical with him. The reality of what's happening to me is coming in waves.

"Can you just tell her one thing for me?"

"Sure."

"Tell her I said, 'I love you.'"

"Sure." He shuts the door.

I walk across the street and sit on a bench facing my apartment. It's raining directly on me as I look up at the second-floor living room windows. The yellow curtains are closed and I can see silhouettes moving around inside. I try and figure out which one is Lila. I realize I forgot to take the garbage out at work, the garbage with Jules' shoes inside. I focus on a pipe that runs alongside the bar underneath my apartment. The water flows off onto the top of a dumpster. My eyes go in and out of focus as I watch the water weep onto the metal.

KEEPING CLEAR

Keep clear
the righteousness of doubt
You're bound to leave
before you know what it's about

Fill up the air
with an idea we all share
The clouds linger over the church
the whole planet plans to plummet

Sick children with cheap fillings
planning their lifetimes
hogtied to fleeting feelings
of real love and free murder
Grow up, face the future
Abandoned homes and student loans
transcend behind the couch
where we'll play with our toys

like we are still little boys

WHERE I GO NEXT

A blessed breeze
pushes me off the tracks
to the trains
like Denis Johnson or
collision consoles
whipping past me,
uncaring
like the past me.

I have nothing left to be afraid of
besides maybe a tumor.
And even then,
I hope I'd sit back with my friend Pat
and seek the humor.
And if it kills me,
my loved ones should know
I died happy, but
mostly annoyed.
And I'll be watching
when you pull out your laptop
and you lock your bedroom door.
When you pull out your tube sock,
I'm judging you.
I'm taking pictures
and I'm laughing at you.
Sitting there with Rooha,
maybe with a lit blunt.
Maybe where I go next
I'm not an addict.
But for now, my mother says
I'm probably healthy.
Google searches disagree
in a world where our god
is broadcast through screens.
All knowing,
all powerful
screens.
Who should I believe?

I still get a dark taste

watching the unthoughtful masses
of clumped-up, spot-cleaned suits.
Pursuing what?
Fancy toothbrushes and
the newest carpet cleaners?
But then my train
ascends and
I look at the Brooklyn Bridge
and the statue who stands so
confused over
what she is meant to represent.
And I'm okay.

You'd be okay, too,
if after ten years of dirt and fog,
you were headed to Central Park
to walk a dog.

ABOUT THE AUTHOR

Niall Power is a fiction writer and poet from New York City.

He has enrolled in and dropped out of The City College of New York three times.

He lives in Brooklyn, New York.

CPSIA information can be obtained
at www.ICGtesting.com
Printed in the USA
BVOW08s0248160118
505308BV00001B/9/P